# Studying
# Sherlock Holmes

EMC Study Guides

# Credits

Written and edited by Kate Oliver

Design: English and Media Centre

Front cover: 'His Last Bow' (George Newnes, 1925), cover design by Frank Wiles
Back cover: 'Sherlock Holmes sees Faces in the Smoke' (William Gillette, 1901)

Printed by: Gutenberg Press

Published by: English and Media Centre, 18 Compton Terrace, London, N1 2UN, © 2004

ISBN: 0 907016 84 7

# Acknowledgements

Thanks to: Danielle Bowe, Acland Burghley School; Patricia Morris, Challney High School for Girls; Afifa Tufail and the English Department at Heart of England School for commenting on, and piloting the material. Also to Barbara Bleiman and Lucy Webster for their comments and suggestions.

Thanks to the following publishers and picture libraries for permission to reproduce copyright material:

The Sherlock Holmes Memorabilia Company for the following images, all © Richard Lancelyn Green Collection, 1992: 'His Last Bow' (George Newnes, 1925), cover design by Frank Wiles, 'Sherlock Holmes sees Faces in the Smoke' (William Gillette, 1901), *The Strand Magazine*, January 1927 'The Retired Colourman', 'H.A. Saintsbury' as Sherlock Holmes (Poster, 1903), 'Holmes gave me a sketch of the events' from 'Silver Blaze'; Clive Brook in *Sherlock Holmes*, d. William K. Howard (1932), Credit: Fox/The Kobal Collection; Nigel Bruce and Basil Rathbone in *Sherlock Holmes: House of Fear*, d. Roy William Neill (1945), Credit: Universal/The Kobal Collection; Andre Morell and Peter Cushing in *The Hound of the Baskervilles*, d. Terence Fisher (1959), Credit: Hammer/The Kobal Collection.

# Further resources

Sherlock Holmes Memorabilia Company 230 Baker Street, London, NW1 5RT,
Tel: 020 7486 1426, www.sh-memorabilia.co.uk, stock postcards, posters, videos, DVDs, books and all things Sherlockian.

# Please note

# Contents      Page

# Teachers' notes

These resources are designed to help students produce a piece of coursework for the pre-1914 prose requirement for English and/or Literature. In the coursework assignments section you will also find a suggestion for an original writing assignment. Four stories are included in the study guide and, although students should *read* at least one other to fulfil the QCA requirements, you will want to check with your exam board how many stories students must *write* about (for example AQA A suggest that students write about a minimum of three stories).

Although written to support pupils studying Sherlock Holmes for GCSE, the objectives and requirements are not referred to explicitly, except in Section 5, so the activities are also suitable for those studying the stories for Standard Grade or Key Stage 3.

The study guide is in five sections.
• Section 1 contains pre-reading activities to give students a 'way in' to the stories.
• Section 2 contains four stories, with suggested activities to do before, during and after reading each story.
• Section 3 contains activities to do after reading several stories.
• Section 4 puts the stories into their social, historical and literary context.
• Section 5 contains suggested coursework assignments and advice for students on planning, writing and re-drafting their work.

As it is unlikely that you will have time to work through all the activities in this study guide, it is suggested that you decide on an assignment title or choice of titles before you begin the unit, and then dip into relevant activities. If you choose one of the titles in the final section of the pack, you will find that a list of relevant activities is suggested for each assignment. If you prefer to write your own assignment title you may find the following chart useful. It will help you to find activities relevant to the title you have created.

| Aspect | Doyle's methods | Location |
|---|---|---|
| Structure | Structure of a crime story | 'A Scandal in Bohemia' (p44); After reading (p88-89) |
| | Openings | 'Silver Blaze' (p15); 'A Scandal in Bohemia' (p30, 31); 'The Red-Headed League' (p50) |
| | Endings | 'A Scandal in Bohemia' ('Why does Holmes fail?' p45-48) |
| | Revealing clues | 'Silver Blaze' (p27); After reading (p90-92) |
| | Building tension | 'The Red-Headed League' (p64); 'The Speckled Band' (p79) |
| Style | Creating atmosphere | 'The Red-Headed League' (p64) |
| | Titles | 'The Red-Headed League' (p49); 'The Speckled Band' (p66) |
| | Description | 'Silver Blaze' (p28-29) |
| | Dialogue | After reading (p95-97) |
| | Humour | 'The Red-Headed League' (p64) |
| Character | Holmes | Before reading (p5-9); 'A Scandal in Bohemia' (p45) 'The Speckled Band' (p81); After reading (p83-85, 90-91) |
| | Watson | 'The Red-Headed League' (p62-63); After reading (p86-87, 93-7) |
| | Relationship between Holmes and Watson | 'The Red-Headed League' (p62); After reading (p95-97) |
| | Irene Adler | 'A Scandal in Bohemia' (p46-48) |
| Point of view | Watson as narrator | 'The Red-Headed League' (p62-63); After reading (p93-94) |
| Context | Genre | 'The Speckled Band' (p66) After reading (p88-89, 98-101) |
| | Attitudes to women | 'A Scandal in Bohemia' (p47) |
| | Attitudes to class & status | After reading (p102-104) |
| | Attitudes to crime & criminals | After reading (p105-6) |
| | Attitudes to scandals | 'A Scandal in Bohemia' (p30, 44) |

# Before reading

## What do you already know about crime fiction?

Crime is a very popular genre, in books, in films and on television.

**As a class, brainstorm the names of any fictional detectives you already know. You could do some research by looking in a television guide.**

**With a partner, choose one detective you have both heard of and brainstorm some more details. Try to include:**

• a description of the detective's personality
• details about how they work for example, do they work alone, or do they have a partner?

**Now feed back to the whole class. Are there any characteristics that many different detectives seem to share? For example, fictional detectives are often loners or rebels and are often obsessive about getting to the truth. Keep your notes from this discussion – they will be helpful later!**

## Introducing Sherlock Holmes

Mr Sherlock Holmes was first introduced to the Victorian public in a short novel called *A Study in Scarlet* in 1887.

### Introducing Holmes – images

**Look at the images of Sherlock Holmes on pages 6 and 7. With a partner discuss what you already know about him and what else you can tell from the images.**

## Representations of Holmes

## Introducing Holmes – extracts

**With a partner, take responsibility for looking at two or three of the extracts (below and on page 9), which are written in the voice of Dr Watson, Holmes's friend and assistant. Make some notes about each one. In your notes you should include the points which follow.**

- Anything that interests or puzzles you.
- What you learn about Sherlock Holmes in each extract.
- Any questions you would like answered.

**Discuss your findings with another pair. Together, make a list of words you could use to describe Holmes.**

---

### Extract 1 – 'A Study in Scarlet'

**Watson first meets Holmes. Holmes has just found a way of testing any brown stain to check whether or not it is blood and tells Watson about his discovery.**

'A man is suspected of a crime, perhaps months after it has been committed. His linen or clothes are examined, and brownish stains discovered upon them. Are they blood stains, or mud stains, or rust stains, or fruit stains, or what are they? That is a question which has puzzled many an expert, and why? Because there was no reliable test. Now we have the Sherlock Holmes test, and there will no longer be any difficulty.'

His eyes fairly glittered as he spoke, and he put his hand over his heart and bowed, as if to some applauding crowd conjured up by his imagination.

---

### Extract 2 – 'The Musgrave Ritual'

An anomaly which often struck me in the character of my friend Sherlock Holmes was that, though in his methods of thought he was the neatest and most methodical of mankind, and although he also affected a certain quiet primness of dress, he was nonetheless in his personal habits the most untidy fellow that ever drove a fellow-lodger to distraction. Not that I am in the least bit conventional in that respect myself ... But with me there is a limit, and when I find a man who keeps his cigars in the coal scuttle, his tobacco in the toe-end of a Persian slipper, and his unanswered correspondence transfixed by a jack-knife into the very centre of his wooden mantelpiece, then I begin to give myself virtuous airs.

---

### Extract 3 – 'The Boscombe Valley Mystery'

Sherlock Holmes was transformed when he was hot upon such a scent as this. Men who had known only the quiet thinker and logician of Baker Street would have failed to recognise him. His face flushed and darkened. His brows were drawn into two hard, black lines, while his eyes shone out from beneath them in a steely glitter ... His nostrils seemed to dilate with a purely animal lust for the chase, and his mind was so absolutely concentrated on the matter before him that a question or remark fell unheeded upon his ears, or at the most provoked only a quick, impatient snarl in reply.

---

### Extract 4 – 'The Adventure of Black Peter'

So unworldly was he – or so capricious – that he frequently refused his help to the powerful and wealthy where the problem made no appeal to his sympathies, while he would devote weeks of most intense application to the affairs of some humble client whose case presented those strange and dramatic qualities which appealed to his imagination and challenged his ingenuity.

## Extract 5 – 'A Scandal in Bohemia'

I had seen little of Holmes lately. My own complete happiness, and the home-centred interests which rise up around the man who first finds himself master of his own establishment, were sufficient to absorb all my attention; while Holmes, who loathed every form of society with his whole Bohemian soul, remained in our lodging in Baker Street, buried among his old books, and alternating from week to week between cocaine and ambition, the drowsiness of the drug, and the fierce energy of his own keen nature. He was still, as ever, deeply attracted by the study of crime, and occupied his immense faculties and extraordinary powers of observation in following out those clues, and clearing up those mysteries, which had been abandoned as hopeless by the official police.

## Extract 6 – 'A Scandal in Bohemia'

'... How do I know that you have been getting yourself very wet lately, and that you have a most clumsy and careless servant girl?'

'My dear Holmes,' said I, 'this is too much. You would certainly have burned if you had lived a few centuries ago. It is true that I had a country walk on Thursday and came home in a dreadful mess; but, as I have changed my clothes, I can't imagine how you deduced it. As to Mary Jane, she is incorrigible, and my wife has given her notice; but there again I fail to see how you work it out.'

He chuckled to himself and rubbed his long nervous hands together.

'It is simplicity itself,' said he; 'my eyes tell me that on the inside of your left shoe, just where the firelight strikes it, the leather is scored by six almost parallel cuts. Obviously they have been caused by someone who has very carelessly scraped round the edges of the sole in order to remove crusted mud from it. Hence, you see, my double deduction that you had been out in vile weather, and that you had a particularly malignant, boot-slitting specimen of the London slavey ...'

## Extract 7 – 'The Noble Batchelor'

'Good day, Lord St Simon,' said Holmes, rising and bowing. 'Pray take the basket chair ... Draw up a little to the fire, and we shall talk this matter over.'

'A most painful matter to me, as you can readily imagine, Mr Holmes. I have been cut to the quick. I understand you have already managed several delicate cases of this sort, sir, though I presume they were hardly from the same class of society.'

'No, I am descending.'

'I beg pardon?'

'My last client of the sort was a king.'

## Extract 8 – 'The Adventure of the Greek Interpreter'

'My dear Watson,' said he, 'I cannot agree with those who rank modesty among the virtues. To the logician all things should be seen exactly as they are, and to underestimate one's self is as much a departure from truth as to exaggerate one's own powers.'

## Extract 9 – 'The Adventure of the Six Napoleons'

Lestrade and I sat silent for a moment, and then, with a spontaneous impulse, we both broke out clapping, as at the well-wrought crisis of a play. A flush of colour sprang to Holmes's pale cheeks, and he bowed to us like the master dramatist who receives the homage of his audience. It was at such moments that, for an instant, he ceased, to be a reasoning machine, and betrayed his human love for admiration and applause. The same singularly proud and reserved nature, which turned away with disdain from popular notoriety, was capable of being moved to its depths by spontaneous wonder and praise from a friend.

# Are you a good detective?

Holmes is particularly famous for the science of 'deduction'. This means looking at clues in a logical way and drawing conclusions from them.

## Making use of clues

**Here are three observations made by Holmes. What would you deduce from each one? In other words, what conclusions would you draw? (The deductions made by Holmes are printed on page 128.)**

**1**

### From 'The Boscombe Valley Mystery'

Holmes observes some muddy ground closely. He notices a set of footprints that seem to belong to the murderer. The prints are far apart and the impression made by the right foot is clearer than the left. He also knows that the murdered man was killed by a heavy blow from behind, to the left side of the head. He finds a stone nearby with grass growing underneath it.

**2**

### From 'A Case of Identity'

Holmes and Watson observe a woman outside on the street.

From under this great panoply* she peeped up in a nervous, hesitating fashion at our windows, while her body oscillated* backwards and forwards, and her fingers fidgeted with her glove buttons. Suddenly, with a plunge, as of a swimmer who leaves the bank, she hurried across the road, and we heard the sharp clang of the bell.

*panoply = he is describing a large, fancy hat*
*oscillated = swung*

**3**

### From 'A Case of Identity'

Holmes explains what he observed about the woman who had come to see him for help.

'I was then much surprised and interested on glancing down to observe that, though the boots which she was wearing were not unlike each other, they were really odd ones, the one having a slightly decorated toe-cap, and the other a plain one. One was buttoned only in the two lower buttons out of five and the other at the first, third, and fifth.'

# Reading the stories

## Some tips

When you are reading more challenging texts, or texts that were written a long time ago, you may worry that you are not understanding them very well. The text might contain difficult vocabulary or refer to things you've never heard of because they are not used anymore. Some words that you *do* know may have changed their meaning: 'gay' used simply to mean 'happy' for example.

Here are some tips for reading the Sherlock Holmes stories.

- RELAX. Accept that there will be lots of words, phrases, sentences and even whole paragraphs you won't understand. Think of the story as a bit of a puzzle.

- If reading difficult texts makes you feel anxious or frustrated, take a few moments before reading to take some deep breaths. Say to yourself: 'I know I won't understand everything, and that's okay.'

- Remember, it is unlikely that *anyone* in the class (even your teacher) will understand everything in the story. It will be difficult for everyone, so work together.

- Once you have started reading, keep going, rather than stopping to look up every word you don't know. If you keep looking things up, it interrupts the flow of your reading and makes it difficult to remember what is happening.

- However, it is a good idea to pause briefly from time to time, to check that you've got the gist of what is happening. Some good points to do this are suggested for you in the text, with questions or activities to help your understanding.

- If possible, listen to someone else read the story while you follow along. Make sure you are listening to someone who understands what they are reading as their tone of voice and expression will help *your* understanding. Your teacher might read to you or you can get audiotapes of people reading many of the Holmes stories. (Ask in a library, in a big bookshop, or search on the web.) And do follow along in the text while the person reads. When the text is going into your brain through both your ears and your eyes it helps your mind to process the information.

- When you've finished the story, make a few notes of all the things you *did* understand. You will probably be surprised at how much of the story you have taken in.

- Compare your notes with someone else – what can you add to each other's understanding? Remember, working together helps.

- Now re-read the story. This time, look up any words that are *really* stopping you from understanding what is happening. If you still feel very confused, ask for help.

# Silver Blaze

## Before reading

### Making use of clues – are you the new Sherlock Holmes?

In this story a valuable race-horse has been stolen from its stable. The police suspect either a band of gypsies who were camping nearby, or a stranger who visited the stable the day before. Sherlock Holmes disagrees with the police inspector who asks:

---

'Is there any other point to which you would draw my attention?'

'To the curious incident of the dog in the night-time.'

'The dog did nothing in the night-time.'

'That was the curious incident,' remarked Sherlock Holmes.

---

**What deductions would you make from this clue?**

**Now read the story to find out if you were right ...**

## During reading

As you read the story you will find that at each **PAUSE** symbol there are questions or activities to help you to check your understanding of the story.

# Silver Blaze

'I am afraid, Watson that I shall have to go,' said Holmes as we sat down together to our breakfast one morning.

'Go! Where to?'

'To Dartmoor – to King's Pyland.'

I was not surprised. Indeed, my only wonder was that he had not already been mixed up in this extraordinary case, which was the one topic of conversation through the length and breadth of England. For a whole day my companion had rambled about the room with his chin upon his chest and his brows knitted, charging and recharging his pipe with the strongest black tobacco, and absolutely deaf to any of my questions or remarks. Fresh editions of every paper had been sent up by our newsagent only to be glanced over and tossed down into a corner. Yet, silent as he was, I knew perfectly well what it was over which he was brooding. There was but one problem before the public which could challenge his powers of analysis, and that was the singular disappearance of the favourite for the Wessex Cup, and the tragic murder of its trainer. When, therefore, he suddenly announced his intention of setting out for the scene of the drama, it was only what I had both expected and hoped for.

'I should be most happy to go down with you if I should not be in the way,' said I.

'My dear Watson, you would confer a great favour upon me by coming. And I think that your time will not be miss-spent, for there are points about the case which promise to make it an absolutely unique one. We have, I think, just time to catch our train at Paddington, and I will go further into the matter upon our journey. You would oblige me by bringing with you your very excellent field-glass.'

---

**PAUSE**       **Think about the opening of the story.**

---

- How does Conan Doyle interest the reader and try to get them to read on?
- What does the opening tell you about the relationship between Holmes and Watson?

And so it happened that an hour or so later I found myself in the corner of a first-class carriage flying along en route for Exeter, while Sherlock Holmes, with his sharp, eager face framed in his ear-flapped travelling-cap, dipped rapidly into the bundle of fresh papers which he had procured at Paddington. We had left Reading far behind us before he thrust the last of them under the seat, and offered me his cigar-case.

'We are going well,' said he, looking out of the window, and glancing at his watch. 'Our rate at present is fifty-three and a half miles an hour.'

'I have not observed the quarter-mile posts,' said I.

'Nor have I. But the telegraph posts upon this line are sixty yards apart, and the calculation is a simple one. I presume that you have looked into this matter of the murder of John Straker and the disappearance of Silver Blaze?'

'I have seen what the *Telegraph* and the *Chronicle* have to say.'

'It is one of those cases where the art of the reasoner should be used rather for the sifting of details than for the acquiring of fresh evidence. The tragedy has been so uncommon, so complete, and of such personal importance to so many people that we are suffering from a plethora of surmise, conjecture, and hypothesis. The difficulty is to detach the framework of fact – of absolute undeniable fact – from the embellishments of theorists and reporters. Then, having established ourselves upon this sound basis, it is our duty to see what inferences may be drawn, and what are the special points upon which the whole mystery turns. On Tuesday evening I received telegrams from both Colonel Ross, the owner of the horse, and from Inspector Gregory, who is looking after the case, inviting my cooperation.'

'Tuesday evening!' I exclaimed. 'And this is Thursday morning. Why did you not go down yesterday?'

'Because I made a blunder, my dear Watson – which is, I am afraid, a more common occurrence than anyone would think who only knew me through your memoirs. The fact is that I could not believe it possible that the most remarkable horse in England could long remain concealed, especially in so sparsely inhabited a place as the north of Dartmoor. From hour to hour yesterday I expected to hear that he had been found, and that his abductor was the murderer of John Straker. When, however, another morning had come and I found that, beyond the arrest of young Fitzroy Simpson, nothing had been done, I felt that it was time for me to take action. Yet in some ways I feel that yesterday has not been wasted.'

'You have formed a theory, then?'

'At least I have got a grip of the essential facts of the case. I shall enumerate them to you, for nothing clears up a case so much as stating it to another person, and I can hardly expect your cooperation if I do not show you the position from which we start.'

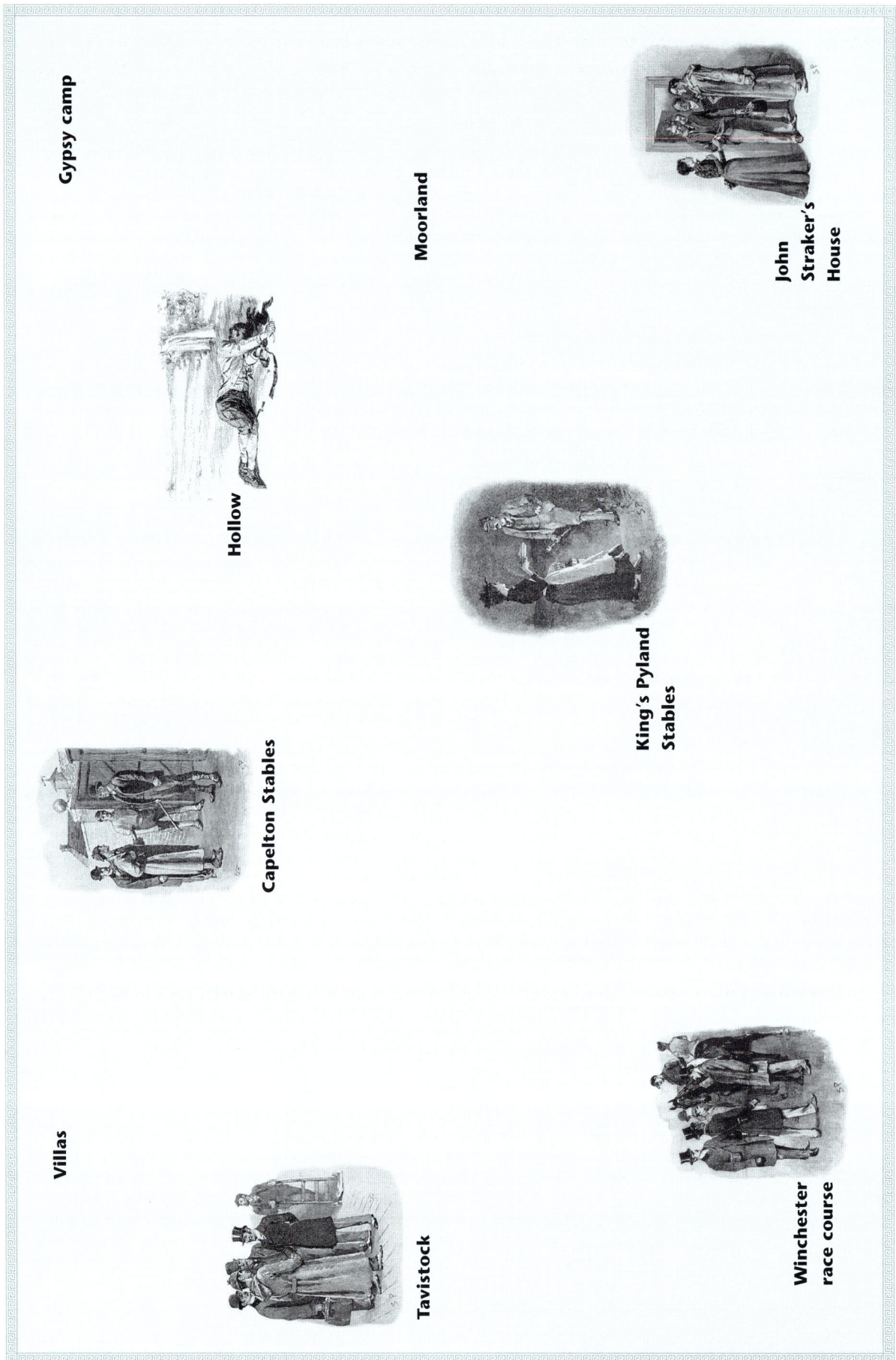

# Map

Gypsy camp

Moorland

Hollow

John
Straker's
House

King's Pyland
Stables

Capelton Stables

Villas

Tavistock

Winchester
race course

I lay back against the cushions, puffing at my cigar, while Holmes, leaning forward, with his long thin forefinger checking off the points upon the palm of his left hand, gave me a sketch of the events which had led to our journey.

**PAUSE** **You are going to keep track of what happens in the story by drawing a map of the locations, following the example on page 14. As you read, add details to your map to show where important events take place and what you have learned about the mystery (a PAUSE sign will tell you when to do this). You should make sure that your map is large enough for you to add, or make changes to, information as you read. By the end of the story your map should show exactly what happened where on the night John Straker died. On your map you should have:**

- the town of Tavistock
- King's Pyland stables, about 2 miles east of Tavistock and surrounded by moorland (a large stretch of wild, open countryside)
- John Straker's house, close to King's Pyland stables
- Capelton stables, about two miles west of King's Pyland (close to Tavistock)
- a group of 'villas' (houses) half a mile to the north of Tavistock
- a dip or hollow in the moor, about a quarter of a mile away from King's Pyland stables
- a gypsy camp, about a mile away from the hollow
- Winchester racetrack (some distance away, to the south).

'Silver Blaze,' said he, 'is from the Isonomy stock, and holds as brilliant a record as his famous ancestor. He is now in his fifth year and has brought in turn each of the prizes of the turf to Colonel Ross, his fortunate owner. Up to the time of the catastrophe he was the first favourite for the Wessex Cup, the betting being three to one on him. He has always, however, been a prime favourite with the racing public, and has never yet disappointed them, so that even at those odds enormous sums of money have been laid upon him. It is obvious, therefore, that there were many people who had the strongest interest in preventing Silver Blaze from being there at the fall of the flag next Tuesday.

'The fact was, of course, appreciated at King's Pyland, where the Colonel's training stable is situated. Every precaution was taken to guard the favourite. The trainer, John Straker, is a retired jockey who rode in Colonel Ross's colours before he became too heavy for the weighing-chair. He has served the Colonel for five years as jockey and for seven as trainer, and has always shown himself to be a zealous and honest servant. Under him were three lads, for the establishment was a small one, containing only four horses in all. One of these lads sat up each night in the stable, while the others slept in the loft. All three bore excellent characters. John Straker, who is a married man, lived in a small villa about two hundred yards from the stables. He has no children, keeps one maidservant, and is comfortably off. The country round is very lonely, but about half a mile to the north there is a small cluster of villas which have been built by a Tavistock contractor for the use of invalids and others who may wish to enjoy the pure Dartmoor air. Tavistock itself lies two miles to the west, while across the moor, also about two miles distant, is the larger training establishment of Capelton, which belongs to Lord Backwater and is managed by Silas Brown. In every other direction the moor is a complete wilderness, inhabited only by a few roaming gypsies. Such was the general situation last Monday night, when the catastrophe occurred.

'On that evening the horses had been exercised and watered as usual, and the stables were locked up at nine o'clock. Two of the lads walked up to the trainer's house, where they had supper in the kitchen, while the third, Ned Hunter, remained on guard. At a few minutes after nine the maid, Edith Baxter, carried down to the stables his supper, which consisted of a dish of curried mutton. She took no liquid, as there was a water-tap in the stables, and it was the rule that the lad on duty should drink nothing else. The maid carried a lantern with her, as it was very dark, and the path ran across the open moor.

'Edith Baxter was within thirty yards of the stables when a man appeared out of the darkness and called to her to stop. As she stepped into the circle of yellow light thrown by the lantern she saw that he was a person of gentlemanly bearing, dressed in a grey suit of tweed, with a cloth cap. He wore gaiters, and carried a heavy stick with a knob to it. She was most impressed, however, by the extreme pallor of his face and by the nervousness of his manner. His age, she thought, would be rather over thirty than under it.

'"Can you tell me where I am?" he asked. "I had almost made up my mind to sleep on the moor when I saw the light of your lantern."

'"You are close to the King's Pyland training stables," she said.

'"Oh, indeed! What a stroke of luck!" he cried. "I understand that a stable boy sleeps there alone every night.

Perhaps that is his supper which you are carrying to him. Now I am sure that you would not be too proud to earn the price of a new dress, would you?" He took a piece of white paper folded up out of his waistcoat pocket. "See that the boy has this tonight, and you shall have the prettiest frock that money can buy."

'She was frightened by the earnestness of his manner, and ran past him to the window through which she was accustomed to hand the meals. It was already open, and Hunter was seated at the small table inside. She had begun to tell him of what had happened, when the stranger came up again.

'"Good evening," said he, looking through the window, "I wanted to have a word with you." The girl has sworn that as he spoke she noticed the corner of the little paper packet protruding from his closed hand.

"What business have you here?" asked the lad.

'"It's business that may put something into your pocket," said the other. "You've two horses in for the Wessex Cup – Silver Blaze and Bayard. Let me have the straight tip, and you won't be a loser. Is it a fact that at the weights Bayard could give the other a hundred yards in five furlongs, and that the stable have put their money on him?"

'"So you're one of those damned touts," cried the lad. "I'll show you how we serve them in King's Pyland." He sprang up and rushed across the stable to unloose the dog. The girl fled away to the house, but as she ran she looked back, and saw that the stranger was leaning through the window. A minute later, however, when Hunter rushed out with the hound he was gone, and though he ran all round the buildings he failed to find any trace of him.'

**PAUSE**  **Add information to your map: where have important events taken place and what have you learned about the mystery?**

'One moment!' I asked. 'Did the stable-boy, when he ran out with the dog, leave the door unlocked behind him?'

'Excellent, Watson; excellent!' murmured my companion. 'The importance of the point struck me so forcibly, that I sent a special wire to Dartmoor yesterday to clear the matter up. The boy locked the door before he left it. The window, I may add, was not large enough for a man to get through.

'Hunter waited until his fellow-grooms had returned, when he sent a message to the trainer and told him what had occurred. Straker was excited at hearing the account, although he does not seem to have quite realized its true significance. It left him, however, vaguely uneasy, and Mrs Straker, waking at one in the morning, found that he was dressing. In reply to her inquiries, he said that he could not sleep on account of his anxiety about the horses, and that he intended to walk down to the stables to see that all was well. She begged him to remain at home, as she could hear the rain pattering against the windows, but in spite of her entreaties he pulled on his large mackintosh and left the house.

'Mrs Straker awoke at seven in the morning, to find that her husband had not yet returned. She dressed herself hastily, called the maid, and set off for the stables. The door was open; inside, huddled together upon a chair, Hunter was sunk in a state of absolute stupor, the favourite's stall was empty, and there were no signs of his trainer.

'The two lads who slept in the chaff-cutting loft above the harness-room were quickly aroused. They had heard nothing during the night, for they are both sound sleepers. Hunter was obviously under the influence of some powerful drug; and, as no sense could be got out of him, he was left to sleep it off while the two lads and the two women ran out in search of the absentees. They still had hopes that the trainer had for some reason taken out the horse for early exercise, but on ascending the knoll near the house, from which all the neighbouring moors were visible, they not only could see no signs of the missing favourite, but they perceived something which warned them that they were in the presence of a tragedy.

'About a quarter of a mile from the stables, John Straker's overcoat was flapping from a furze bush. Immediately beyond there was a bowl-shaped depression in the moor, and at the bottom of this was found the dead body of the unfortunate trainer. His head had been shattered by a savage blow from some heavy weapon, and he was wounded in the thigh, where there was a long, clean cut, inflicted evidently by some very sharp instrument. It was clear, however, that Straker had defended himself vigorously against his assailants, for in his right hand he held a small knife, which was clotted with blood up to the handle, while in his left he clasped a red and black silk cravat, which was recognized by the maid as having been worn on the preceding evening by the stranger who had visited the stables.

'Hunter, on recovering from his stupor, was also quite positive as to the ownership of the cravat. He was equally certain that the same stranger had, while standing at the window, drugged his curried mutton, and so deprived the stables of their watchman.

'As to the missing horse, there were abundant proofs in the mud which lay at the bottom of the fatal hollow, that he had been there at the time of the struggle. But from that morning he has disappeared; and although a large reward has been offered, and all the gypsies of Dartmoor are on the alert, no news has come of him.

Finally an analysis has shown that the remains of his supper left by the stable lad contain an appreciable quantity of powdered opium, while the people at the house partook of the same dish on the same night without any ill effect.

**PAUSE**     **Add information to your map.**

'Those are the main facts of the case, stripped of all surmise, and stated as baldly as possible. I shall now recapitulate what the police have done in the matter.

'Inspector Gregory, to whom the case has been committed, is an extremely competent officer. Were he but gifted with imagination he might rise to great heights in his profession. On his arrival he promptly found and arrested the man upon whom suspicion naturally rested. There was little difficulty in finding him, for he inhabited one of those villas which I have mentioned. His name, it appears, was Fitzroy Simpson. He was a man of excellent birth and education, who had squandered a fortune upon the turf, and who lived now by doing a little quiet and genteel bookmaking in the sporting clubs of London. An examination of his betting-book shows that bets to the amount of five thousand pounds had been registered by him against the favourite.

'On being arrested he volunteered the statement that he had come down to Dartmoor in the hope of getting some information about the King's Pyland horses, and also about Desborough, the second favourite, which was in charge of Silas Brown at the Capelton stables. He did not attempt to deny that he had acted as described upon the evening before, but declared that he had no sinister designs, and had simply wished to obtain first-hand information. When confronted with his cravat he turned very pale, and was utterly unable to account for its presence in the hand of the murdered man. His wet clothing showed that he had been out in the storm of the night before, and his stick, which was a Penang lawyer* weighted with lead, was just such a weapon as might, by repeated blows, have inflicted the terrible injuries to which the trainer had succumbed.

'On the other hand, there was no wound upon his person, while the state of Straker's knife would show that one at least of his assailants must bear his mark upon him. There you have it all in a nutshell, Watson, and if you can give me any light I shall be infinitely obliged to you.'

* A kind of walking stick

**PAUSE**     **Discuss your theories about the case so far. You might want to consider what you know about the way stories work – do you expect that the suspect arrested by the police will turn out to have been the murderer? Why or why not?**

I had listened with the greatest interest to the statement which Holmes, with characteristic clearness, had laid before me. Though most of the facts were familiar to me, I had not sufficiently appreciated their relative importance, nor their connection with each other.

'Is it not possible,' I suggested, 'that the incised wound upon Straker may have been caused by his own knife in the convulsive struggles which follow any brain injury?'

'It is more than possible; it is probable,' said Holmes. 'In that case one of the main points in favour of the accused disappears.'

'And yet,' said I, 'even now I fail to understand what the theory of the police can be.'

'I am afraid that whatever theory we state has very grave objections to it,' returned my companion. 'The police imagine, I take it, that this Fitzroy Simpson, having drugged the lad, and having in some way obtained a duplicate key, opened the stable door and took out the horse, with the intention, apparently, of kidnapping him altogether. His bridle is missing, so that Simpson must have put it on. Then, having left the door open behind him, he was leading the horse away over the moor, when he was either met or overtaken by the trainer. A row naturally ensued, Simpson beat out the trainer's brains with his heavy stick without receiving any injury from the small knife which Straker used in self-defence, and then the thief either led the horse on to some secret hiding-place, or else it may have bolted during the struggle, and be now wandering out on the moors. That is the case as it appears to the police, and improbable as it is, all other explanations are more improbable still. However, I shall very quickly test the matter when I am once upon the spot, and until then I cannot really see how we can get much further than our present position.'

It was evening before we reached the little town of Tavistock, which lies, like the boss of a shield, in the middle of the huge circle of Dartmoor. Two gentlemen were awaiting us in the station – the one a tall, fair man with lion-like hair and beard, and curiously penetrating light blue eyes, the other a small alert person, very neat and dapper, in a frock-coat and gaiters, with trim little side-whiskers and an eye-glass. The latter was Colonel Ross, the well-known sportsman, the other, Inspector Gregory, a man who was rapidly making his name in the English detective service.

'I am delighted that you have come down, Mr Holmes,' said the Colonel. 'The Inspector here has done all that could possibly be suggested; but I wish to leave no stone unturned in trying to avenge poor Straker, and in recovering my horse.'

'Have there been any fresh developments?' asked Holmes.

'I am sorry to say that we have made very little progress,' said the Inspector. 'We have an open carriage outside, and as you would no doubt like to see the place before the light fails, we might talk it over as we drive.'

A minute later we were all seated in a comfortable landau and were rattling through the quaint old Devonshire town. Inspector Gregory was full of his case, and poured out a stream of remarks, while Holmes threw in an occasional question or interjection. Colonel Ross leaned back with his arms folded and his hat tilted over his eyes, while I listened with interest to the dialogue of the two detectives. Gregory was formulating his theory, which was almost exactly what Holmes had foretold in the train.

'The net is drawn pretty close round Fitzroy Simpson,' he remarked, 'and I believe myself that he is our man. At the same time I recognize that the evidence is purely circumstantial, and that some new development may upset it.'

'How about Straker's knife?'

'We have quite come to the conclusion that he wounded himself in his fall.'

'My friend Dr Watson made that suggestion to me as we came down. If so, it would tell against this man Simpson.'

'Undoubtedly. He has neither a knife nor any sign of a wound. The evidence against him is certainly very strong. He had a great interest in the disappearance of the favourite, he lies under suspicion of having poisoned the stable boy, he was undoubtedly out in the storm, he was armed with a heavy stick, and his cravat was found in the dead man's hand. I really think we have enough to go before a jury.'

Holmes shook his head. 'A clever counsel would tear it all to rags,' said he. 'Why should he take the horse out of the stable? If he wished to injure it, why could he not do it there? Has a duplicate key been found in his possession? What chemist sold him the powdered opium? Above all, where could he, a stranger to the district, hide a horse, and such a horse as this? What is his own explanation as to the paper which he wished the maid to give to the stable boy?'

'He says that it was a ten-pound note. One was found in his purse. But your other difficulties are not so formidable as they seem. He is not a stranger to the district. He has twice lodged at Tavistock in the summer. The opium was probably brought from London. The key, having served its purpose, would be hurled away. The horse may be at the bottom of one of the pits or old mines upon the moor.'

'What does he say about the cravat?'

'He acknowledges that it is his, and declares that he had lost it. But a new element has been introduced into the case which may account for his leading the horse from the stable.'

Holmes pricked up his ears.

'We have found traces which show that a party of gypsies encamped on Monday night within a mile of the spot where the murder took place. On Tuesday they were gone. Now, presuming that there was some understanding between Simpson and these gypsies, might he not have been leading the horse to them when he was overtaken, and may they not have him now?'

'It is certainly possible.'

'The moor is being scoured for these gypsies. I have also examined every stable and outhouse in Tavistock, and for a radius of ten miles.'

'There is another training stable quite close, I understand?'

'Yes, and that is a factor which we must certainly not neglect. As Desborough, their horse, was second in the betting, they had an interest in the disappearance of the favourite. Silas Brown, the trainer, is known to have had large bets upon the event, and he was no friend to poor Straker. We have, however, examined the stables, and there is nothing to connect him with the affair.'

'And nothing to connect this man Simpson with the interests of the Capelton stable?'

'Nothing at all.'

---

**PAUSE**   **Add information to your map.**

---

Holmes leaned back in the carriage, and the conversation ceased. A few minutes later our driver pulled up at a neat little red-brick villa with overhanging eaves, which stood by the road. Some distance off, across a paddock, lay a long grey-tiled outbuilding. In every other direction the low curves of the moor, bronze-coloured from the fading ferns, stretched away to the skyline, broken only by the steeples of Tavistock, and by a cluster of houses away to the westward which marked the Capelton stables. We all sprang out with the exception of Holmes, who continued to lean back with his eyes fixed upon the sky in front of him, entirely absorbed in his own thoughts. It was only when I touched his arm that he roused himself with a violent start and stepped out of the carriage.

'Excuse me,' said he, turning to Colonel Ross, who had looked at him in some surprise. 'I was day-dreaming.' There was a gleam in his eyes and a suppressed excitement in his manner which convinced me, used as I was to his ways, that his hand was upon a clue, though I could not imagine where he had found it.

'Perhaps you would prefer at once to go on to the scene of the crime, Mr Holmes?' said Gregory.

'I think that I should prefer to stay here a little and go into one or two questions of detail. Straker was brought back here, I presume?'

'Yes, he lies upstairs. The inquest is tomorrow.'

'He has been in your service some years, Colonel Ross?'

'I have always found him an excellent servant.'

'I presume that you made an inventory of what he had in his pockets at the time of his death, Inspector?'

'I have the things themselves in the sitting-room, if you would care to see them.'

'I should be very glad.' We all filed into the front room, and sat round the central table, while the Inspector unlocked a square tin box and laid a small heap of things before us. There was a box of vestas*, two inches of tallow candle. an A D P brier-root pipe, a pouch of sealskin with half an ounce of long-cut Cavendish*, a silver watch with a gold chain, five sovereigns in gold, an aluminium pencil-case, a few papers, and an ivory-handled knife with a very delicate, inflexible blade marked Weiss & Co., London.

'This is a very singular knife,' said Holmes, lifting it up and examining it minutely. 'I presume, as I see blood-stains upon it, that it is the one which was found in the dead man's grasp. Watson, this knife is surely in your line.'

'It is what we call a cataract knife,' said I.

'I thought so. A very delicate blade devised for very delicate work. A strange thing for a man to carry with him upon a rough expedition, especially as it would not shut in his pocket.'

'The tip was guarded by a disc of cork which we found beside his body,' said the Inspector. 'His wife tells us that the knife had lain upon the dressing-table, and that he had picked it up as he left the room. It was a poor weapon, but perhaps the best that he could lay his hands on at the moment.'

'Very possibly. How about these papers?'

'Three of them are receipted hay-dealers' accounts. One of them is a letter of instructions from Colonel Ross. This other is a milliner's account for thirty-seven pounds fifteen, made out by Madame Lesurier, of Bond Street, to William Derbyshire. Mrs Straker tells us that Derbyshire was a friend of her husband's, and that occasionally his letters were addressed here.'

'Madame Derbyshire had somewhat expensive tastes,' remarked Holmes, glancing down the account. 'Twenty-two guineas is rather heavy for a single costume. However, there appears to be nothing more to learn, and we may now go down to the scene of the crime.'

As we emerged from the sitting-room a woman who had been waiting in the passage, took a step forward and laid her hand upon the Inspector's sleeve. Her face was haggard, and thin, and eager, stamped with the print of a recent horror.

'Have you got them? Have you found them?' she panted.

'No, Mrs Straker; but Mr Holmes, here, has come from London to help us, and we shall do all that is possible.'

'Surely I met you in Plymouth, at a garden-party, some little time ago, Mrs Straker?' said Holmes.

'No, sir; you are mistaken.'

'Dear me; why, I could have sworn to it. You wore a costume of dove-coloured silk with ostrich-feather trimming.'

'I never had such a dress, sir,' answered the lady.

'Ah, that quite settles it,' said Holmes; and with an apology he followed the Inspector outside.

* *vestas = matches; Cavendish = tobacco*

**PAUSE**  **Discuss what you think Holmes hopes to learn from this conversation with Mrs Straker.**

**Add information to your map.**

A short walk across the moor took us to the hollow in which the body had been found. At the brink of it was the furze-bush upon which the coat had been hung.

'There was no wind that night, I understand,' said Holmes.

'None, but very heavy rain.'

'In that case the overcoat was not blown against the furze bushes, but placed there.'

'Yes, it was laid across the bush.'

'You fill me with interest. I perceive that the ground has been trampled up a good deal. No doubt many feet have been there since Monday night.'

'A piece of matting has been laid here at the side, and we have all stood upon that.'

'Excellent.'

'In this bag I have one of the boots which Straker wore, one of Fitzroy Simpson's shoes, and a cast horseshoe of Silver Blaze.'

'My dear Inspector, you surpass yourself!'

Holmes took the bag, and descending into the hollow, he pushed the matting into a more central position. Then stretching himself upon his face and leaning his chin upon his hands, he made a careful study of the trampled mud in front of him.

'Halloa!' said he, suddenly, 'what's this?'

It was a wax vesta, half burned, which was so coated with mud that it looked at first like a little chip of wood.

'I cannot think how I came to overlook it,' said the Inspector, with an expression of annoyance.

'It was invisible, buried in the mud. I only saw it because I was looking for it.'

'What! You expected to find it?'

'I thought it not unlikely.' He took the boots from the bag and compared the impressions of each of them with marks upon the ground. Then he clambered up to the rim of the hollow and crawled about among the ferns and bushes.

'I am afraid that there are no more tracks,' said the Inspector. 'I have examined the ground very carefully for a hundred yards in each direction.'

'Indeed!' said Holmes, rising. 'I should not have the impertinence to do it again after what you say. But I should like to take a little walk over the moor before it grows dark that I may know my ground tomorrow, and I think that I shall put this horseshoe into my pocket for luck.'

Colonel Ross, who had shown some signs of impatience at my companion's quiet and systematic method of work, glanced at his watch.

'I wish you would come back with me, Inspector,' said he. 'There are several points on which I should like your advice, and especially as to whether we do not owe it to the public to remove our horse's name from the entries for the cup.'

'Certainly not,' cried Holmes with decision. 'I should let the name stand.'

The Colonel bowed. 'I am very glad to have had your opinion, sir,' said he. 'You will find us at poor Straker's house when you have finished your walk, and we can drive together into Tavistock.'

He turned back with the Inspector, while Holmes and I walked slowly across the moor. The sun was beginning to sink behind the stable of Capelton, and the long sloping plain in front of us was tinged with gold, deepening into rich, ruddy brown where the faded ferns and brambles caught the evening light. But the glories of the landscape were all wasted upon my companion, who was sunk in the deepest thought.

'It's this way, Watson,' he said, at last. 'We may leave the question of who killed John Straker for the instant, and confine ourselves to finding out what has become of the horse. Now, supposing that he broke away during or after the tragedy, where could he have gone to? The horse is a very gregarious creature. If left to himself his instincts would have been either to return to King's Pyland or go over to Capelton. Why should he run wild upon the moor? He would surely have been seen by now. And why should gypsies kidnap him? These people always clear out when they hear of trouble, for they do not wish to be pestered by the police. They could not hope to sell such a horse. They would run a great risk and gain nothing by taking him. Surely that is clear.'

'Where is he, then?'

'I have already said that he must have gone to King's Pyland or to Capelton. He is not at King's Pyland; therefore he is at Capelton. Let us take that as a working hypothesis, and see what it leads us to. This part of the moor, as the Inspector remarked, is very hard and dry. But it falls away towards Capelton, and you can see from here that there is a long hollow over yonder, which must have been very wet on Monday night. If our supposition is correct, then the horse must have crossed that, and there is the point where we should look for his tracks.'

We had been walking briskly during this conversation, and a few more minutes brought us to the hollow in question. At Holmes's request I walked down the bank to the right, and he to the left, but I had not taken fifty paces before I heard him give a shout, and saw him waving his hand to me. The track of a horse was plainly outlined in the soft earth in front of him, and the shoe which he took from his pocket exactly fitted the impression.

'See the value of imagination,' said Holmes. 'It is the one quality which Gregory lacks. We imagined what might have happened, acted upon the supposition, and find ourselves justified. Let us proceed.'

**PAUSE**     **What have you learned about Holmes's methods? Make a note of your ideas, as they will be useful later.**

**Add information to your map.**

We crossed the marshy bottom and passed over a quarter of a mile of dry, hard turf. Again the ground sloped, and again we came on the tracks. Then we lost them for half a mile, but only to pick them up once more quite close to Capelton. It was Holmes who saw them first, and he stood pointing with a look of triumph upon his face. A man's track was visible beside the horse's.

'The horse was alone before,' I cried.

'Quite so. It was alone before. Halloa! what is this?'

The double track turned sharp off and took the direction of King's Pyland. Holmes whistled, and we both followed along after it. His eyes were on the trail, but I happened to look a little to one side and saw to my surprise the same tracks coming back again in the opposite direction.

'One for you, Watson,' said Holmes when I pointed it out; 'you have saved us a long walk, which would have brought us back on our own traces. Let us follow the return track.'

We had not to go far. It ended at the paving of asphalt which led up to the gates of the Capelton stables. As we approached, a groom ran out from them.

'We don't want any loiterers about here,' said he.

'I only wished to ask a question,' said Holmes, with his finger and thumb in his waistcoat pocket. 'Should I be too early to see your master, Mr Silas Brown, if I were to call at five o'clock tomorrow morning?'

'Bless you, sir, if anyone is about he will be, for he is always the first stirring. But here he is, sir, to answer your questions for himself. No, sir, no, it is as much as my place is worth to let him see me touch your money. Afterwards, if you like.'

As Sherlock Holmes replaced the half-crown which he had drawn from his pocket, a fierce-looking elderly man strode out from the gate with a hunting-crop swinging in his hand.

'What's this, Dawson?' he cried. 'No gossiping! Go about your business! And you – what the devil do you want here?'

'Ten minutes' talk with you, my good sir,' said Holmes, in the sweetest of voices.

'I've no time to talk to every gadabout. We want no strangers here. Be off, or you may find a dog at your heels.'

'BE OFF'

Holmes leaned forward and whispered something in the trainer's ear. He started violently and flushed to the temples.

'It's a lie!' he shouted. 'An infernal lie!'

'Very good. Shall we argue about it here in public or talk it over in your parlour?'

'Oh, come in if you wish to.'

Holmes smiled. 'I shall not keep you more than a few minutes, Watson,' he said. 'Now, Mr Brown. I am quite at your disposal.'

It was quite twenty minutes, and the reds had all faded into greys before Holmes and the trainer reappeared. Never have I seen such a change as had been brought about in Silas Brown in that short time. His face was ashy pale, beads of perspiration shone upon his brow, and his hands shook until the hunting-crop wagged like a branch in the wind. His bullying, overbearing manner was all gone too, and he cringed along at my companion's side like a dog with its master.

'Your instructions will be done. It shall all be done,' said he.

'There must be no mistake,' said Holmes, looking round at him. The other winced as he read the menace in his eyes.

'Oh, no, there shall be no mistake. It shall be there. Should I change it first or not?'

Holmes thought a little and then burst out laughing. 'No, don't,' said he, 'I shall write to you about it. No tricks, now, or –'

'Oh, you can trust me, you can trust me!'

'You must see to it on the day as if it were your own.'

'You can rely upon me.'

'Yes, I think I can. Well, you shall hear from me tomorrow.' He turned upon his heel, disregarding the trembling hand which the other held out to him, and we set off for King's Pyland.

'A more perfect compound of the bully, coward and sneak than Master Silas Brown I have seldom met with,' remarked Holmes as we trudged along together.

'He has the horse, then?'

'He tried to bluster out of it, but I described to him so exactly what his actions had been upon that morning, that he is convinced that I was watching him. Of course you observed the peculiarly square toes in the impressions, and that his own boots exactly corresponded to them. Again, of course, no subordinate would have dared to have done such a thing. I described to him how when, according to his custom he was the first down, he perceived a strange horse wandering over the moor; how he went out to it, and his astonishment at recognizing from the white forehead which has given the favourite its name that chance had put in his power the only horse which could beat the one upon which he had put his money. Then I described how his first impulse had been to lead him back to King's Pyland, and how the devil had shown him how he could hide the horse until the race was over, and how he had led it back and concealed it at Capelton. When I told him every detail he gave it up, and thought only of saving his own skin.'

'But his stables had been searched?'

'Oh, an old horse-faker like him has many a dodge.'

'But are you not afraid to leave the horse in his power now, since he has every interest in injuring it?'

'My dear fellow, he will guard it as the apple of his eye. He knows that his only hope of mercy is to produce it safe.'

'Colonel Ross did not impress me as a man who would be likely to show much mercy in any case.'

'The matter does not rest with Colonel Ross. I follow my own methods, and tell as much or as little as I choose. That is the advantage of being unofficial. I don't know whether you observed it, Watson, but the Colonel's manner has been just a trifle cavalier to me. I am inclined now to have a little amusement at his expense. Say nothing to him about the horse.'

'Certainly not without your permission.'

| PAUSE | Discuss what you think you learn about Holmes from the way he reacts to Colonel Ross. |
|---|---|
| | Add information to your map. |

'And, of course, this is all quite a minor point compared to the question of who killed John Straker.'

'And you will devote yourself to that?'

'On the contrary, we both go back to London by the night train.'

I was thunderstruck by my friend's words. We had only been a few hours in Devonshire, and that he should give up an investigation which he had begun so brilliantly was quite incomprehensible to me. Not a word more could I draw from him until we were back at the trainer's house. The Colonel and the Inspector were awaiting us in the parlour.

'My friend and I return to town by the midnight express,' said Holmes. 'We have had a charming little breath of your beautiful Dartmoor air.'

The Inspector opened his eyes, and the Colonel's lip curled in a sneer.

'So you despair of arresting the murderer of poor Straker,' said he.

Holmes shrugged his shoulders. 'There are certainly grave difficulties in the way,' said he. 'I have every hope, however, that your horse will start upon Tuesday, and I beg that you will have your jockey in readiness. Might I ask for a photograph of Mr John Straker?'

The Inspector took one from an envelope and handed it to him.

'My dear Gregory, you anticipate all my wants. If I might ask you to wait here for an instant, I have a question which I should like to put to the maid.'

'I must say that I am rather disappointed in our London consultant,' said Colonel Ross, bluntly, as my friend left the room. 'I do not see that we are any further than when he came.'

'At least you have his assurance that your horse will run,' said I.

'Yes, I have his assurance,' said the Colonel, with a shrug of his shoulders. 'I should prefer to have the horse.'

I was about to make some reply in defence of my friend, when he entered the room again.

'Now, gentlemen,' said he, 'I am quite ready for Tavistock.'

As we stepped into the carriage one of the stable lads held the door open for us. A sudden idea seemed to occur to Holmes, for he leaned forward and touched the lad upon the sleeve.

'You have a few sheep in the paddock,' he said. 'Who attends to them?'

'I do, sir.'

'Have you noticed anything amiss with them of late?'

'Well, sir, not of much account, but three of them have gone lame, sir.'

I could see that Holmes was extremely pleased, for he chuckled and rubbed his hands together.

'A long shot, Watson, a very long shot!' said he, pinching my arm. 'Gregory, let me recommend to your attention this singular epidemic among the sheep. Drive on, coachman!'

Colonel Ross still wore an expression which showed the poor opinion which he had formed of my companion's ability, but I saw by the Inspector's face that his attention had been keenly aroused.

'You consider that to be important?' he asked.

'Exceedingly so.'

'Is there any point to which you would wish to draw my attention?'

'To the curious incident of the dog in the night-time.'

'The dog did nothing in the night-time.'

'That was the curious incident,' remarked Sherlock Holmes.

---

**PAUSE**          **Add information to your map.**

---

Four days later Holmes and I were again in the train, bound for Winchester, to see the race for the Wessex Cup. Colonel Ross met us, by appointment, outside the station, and we drove in his drag* to the course beyond the town. His face was grave, and his manner was cold in the extreme.

'I have seen nothing of my horse,' said he.

'I suppose that you would know him when you saw him?' asked Holmes.

The Colonel was very angry. 'I have been on the turf for twenty years and never was asked such a question as that before,' said he. 'A child would know Silver Blaze with his white forehead and his mottled off foreleg.'

*\* A private horse-drawn coach*

'How is the betting?'

'Well, that is the curious part of it. You could have got fifteen to one yesterday, but the price has become shorter and shorter, until you can hardly get three to one now.'

'Hum!' said Holmes. 'Somebody knows something, that is clear!'

As the drag drew up in the enclosure near the grandstand I glanced at the card to see the entries. It ran:

Wessex Plate. 50 sovs. Each, h ft, with one thousand sovs. added, for four-and five-year olds. Second, £300. Third, £200. New course (one mile and five furlongs).

1. Mr Heath Newton's The Negro (red cap, cinnamon jacket).
2. Colonel Wardlaw's Pugilist (pink cap, blue and black jacket).
3. Lord Backwater's Desborough (yellow cap and sleeves).
4. Colonel Ross's Silver Blaze (black cap, red jacket).
5. Duke of Balmoral's Iris (yellow and black stripes).
6. Lord Singleford's Rasper (purple cap, black sleeves).

'We scratched our other one and put all hopes on your word,' said the Colonel. 'Why, what is that? Silver Blaze favourite?'

'Five to four against Silver Blaze!' roared the ring. 'Five to four against Silver Blaze! Fifteen to five against Desborough! Five to four on the field!'

'There are the numbers up,' I cried. 'They are all six there.'

'All six there? Then my horse is running,' cried the Colonel in great agitation. 'But I don't see him. My colours have not passed.'

'Only five have passed. This must be he.'

As I spoke a powerful bay horse swept out from the weighing enclosure and cantered past us, bearing on its back the well-known black and red of the Colonel.

'That's not my horse,' cried the owner. 'That beast has not a white hair upon its body. What is this that you have done, Mr Holmes?'

'Well, well, let us see how he gets on,' said my friend imperturbably. For a few minutes he gazed through my field-glass. 'Capital! An excellent start!' he cried suddenly. 'There they are, coming round the curve!'

From our drag we had a superb view as they came up the straight. The six horses were so close together that a carpet could have covered them, but half-way up the yellow of the Capelton stable showed to the front. Before they reached us, however, Desborough's bolt was shot, and the Colonel's horse, coming away with a rush, passed the post a good six lengths before its rival, the Duke of Balmoral's Iris making a bad third.

'It's my race, anyhow,' gasped the Colonel, passing his hand over his eyes. 'I confess that I can make neither head nor tail of it. Don't you think that you have kept up your mystery long enough, Mr Holmes?'

'Certainly, Colonel. You shall know everything. Let us all go round and have a look at the horse together. Here he is,' he continued as we made our way into the weighing enclosure, where only owners and their friends find admittance. 'You have only to wash his face and his leg in spirits of wine, and you will find that he is the same old Silver Blaze as ever.'

'You take my breath away!'

'I found him in the hands of a faker and took the liberty of running him just as he was sent over.'

'My dear sir, you have done wonders. The horse looks very fit and well. It never went better in its life. I owe you a thousand apologies for having doubted your ability. You have done me a great service by recovering my horse. You would do me a greater still if you could lay your hands on the murderer of John Straker.'

'I have done so,' said Holmes quietly.

The Colonel and I stared at him in amazement. 'You have got him! Where is he, then?'

'He is here.'

'Here! Where?'

'In my company at the present moment.'

The Colonel flushed angrily. 'I quite recognize that I am under obligations to you, Mr Holmes,' said he, 'but I must regard what you have just said as either a very bad joke or an insult.'

Sherlock Holmes laughed. 'I assure you that I have not associated you with the crime, Colonel,' said he; 'The real murderer is standing immediately behind you.' He stepped past and laid his hand upon the glossy neck of the thoroughbred.

'The horse!' cried both the Colonel and myself.

'Yes, the horse. And it may lessen his guilt if I say that it was done in self-defence, and that John Straker was a man who was entirely unworthy of your confidence. But there goes the bell; and as I stand to win a little on this next race, I shall defer a lengthy explanation until a more fitting time.'

HE LAID HIS HAND UPON THE GLOSSY NECK

We had the corner of a Pullman car to ourselves that evening as we whirled back to London, and I fancy that the journey was a short one to Colonel Ross as well as to myself as we listened to our companion's narrative of the events which had occurred at the Dartmoor training-stables upon that Monday night, and the means by which he had unravelled them.

'I confess,' said he, 'that any theories which I had formed from the newspaper reports were entirely erroneous. And yet there were indications there, had they not been overlaid by other details which concealed their true import. I went to Devonshire with the conviction that Fitzroy Simpson was the true culprit, although, of course, I saw that the evidence against him was by no means complete.

'It was while I was in the carriage, just as we reached the trainer's house, that the immense significance of the curried mutton occurred to me. You may remember that I was distrait, and remained sitting after you had all alighted. I was marvelling in my own mind how I could possibly have overlooked so obvious a clue.'

'I confess,' said the Colonel, 'that even now I cannot see how it helps us.'

'It was the first link in my chain of reasoning. Powdered opium is by no means tasteless. The flavour is not disagreeable, but it is perceptible. Were it mixed with any ordinary dish the eater would undoubtedly detect it, and would probably eat no more. A curry was exactly the medium which would disguise this taste. By no possible supposition could this stranger, Fitzroy Simpson, have caused curry to be served in the trainer's family that night, and it is surely too monstrous a coincidence to suppose that he happened to come along with powdered opium upon the very night when a dish happened to be served which would disguise the flavour. That is unthinkable. Therefore Simpson becomes eliminated from the case, and our attention centres upon Straker and his wife, the only two people who could have chosen curried mutton for supper that night. The opium was added after the dish was set aside for the stable boy, for the others had the same for supper with no ill effects. Which of them, then, had access to that dish without the maid seeing them?

'Before deciding that question I had grasped the significance of the silence of the dog, for one true inference invariably suggests others. The Simpson incident had shown me that a dog was kept in the stables, and yet, though someone had been in and had fetched out a horse, he had not barked enough to arouse the two lads in the loft. Obviously the midnight visitor was someone whom the dog knew well.

'I was already convinced, or almost convinced, that John Straker went down to the stables in the dead of the night and took out Silver Blaze. For what purpose? For a dishonest one, obviously, or why should he drug his own stable boy? And yet I was at a loss to know why. There have been cases before now where trainers have made sure of great sums of money by laying against their own horses, through agents, and then preventing them from winning by fraud. Sometimes it is a pulling jockey. Sometimes it is some surer and subtler means. What was it here? I hoped that the contents of his pockets might help me to form a conclusion.

'And they did so. You cannot have forgotten the singular knife which was found in the dead man's hand, a knife which certainly no sane man would choose for a weapon. It was, as Dr Watson told us, a form of knife which is used for the most delicate operations known in surgery. And it was to be used for a delicate operation that night. You must know, with your wide experience of turf matters, Colonel Ross, that it is possible to make a slight nick upon the tendons of a horse's ham, and to do it subcutaneously, so as to leave absolutely no trace. A horse so treated would develop a slight lameness which would be put down to a strain in exercise or a touch of rheumatism, but never to foul play.'

'Villain! Scoundrel!' cried the Colonel.

'We have here the explanation of why John Straker wished to take the horse out on to the moor. So spirited a creature would have certainly roused the soundest of sleepers when it felt the prick of the knife. It was absolutely necessary to do it in the open air.'

'I have been blind!' cried the Colonel. 'Of course that was why he needed the candle and struck the match.'

'Undoubtedly. But in examining his belongings, I was fortunate enough to discover, not only the method of the crime, but even its motives. As a man of the world, Colonel, you know that men do not carry other people's bills about in their pockets. We have most of us quite enough to do to settle our own. I at once concluded that Straker was leading a double life and keeping a second establishment. The nature of the bill showed that there was a lady in the case, and one who had expensive tastes. Liberal as you are with your servants, one can hardly expect that they can buy twenty-guinea walking dresses for their women. I questioned Mrs Straker as to the dress without her knowing it, and having satisfied myself that it had never reached her, I made a note of the milliner's address and felt that by calling there with Straker's photograph, I could easily dispose of the mythical Derbyshire.

'From that time on all was plain. Straker had led out the horse to a hollow where his light would be invisible. Simpson, in his flight, had dropped his cravat, and Straker had picked it up – with some idea, perhaps, that he might use it in securing the horse's leg. Once in the hollow, he had got behind the horse and had struck a light; but the creature, frightened at the sudden glare, and with the strange instinct of animals feeling that some mischief was intended, had lashed out, and the steel shoe had struck Straker full on the forehead. He had already, in spite of the rain, taken off his overcoat in order to do his delicate task, and so, as he fell, his knife gashed his thigh. Do I make it clear?'

'Wonderful!' cried the Colonel. 'Wonderful! You might have been there.'

'My final shot was, I confess, a very long one. It struck me that so astute a man as Straker would not undertake this delicate tendon-nicking without a little practise. What could he practise on? My eyes fell upon the sheep, and I asked a question which, rather to my surprise, showed that my surmise was correct.

'When I returned to London I called upon the milliner, who had recognized Straker as an excellent customer, of the name of Derbyshire, who had a very dashing wife, with a strong partiality for expensive dresses. I have no doubt that this woman had plunged him over head and ears in debt, and so led him into this miserable plot.'

'You have explained all but one thing,' cried the Colonel. 'Where was the horse?'

'Ah, it bolted and was cared for by one of your neighbours. We must have an amnesty in that direction, I think. This is Clapham Junction, if I am not mistaken, and we shall be in Victoria in less than ten minutes. If you care to smoke a cigar in our rooms, Colonel. I shall be happy to give you any other details which might interest you.'

---

**Up-date your map so that it now shows exactly what happened where on the night John Straker died. Compare your map with those of other people in the class. Do your versions of events agree? If not, check back in the story to see who is right and correct your map if necessary.**

---

# After reading

## Your personal response

With your partner, discuss the questions listed below.

- What did you like about the story? What didn't you like?
- Remind yourself of the work you did before reading, brainstorming ideas about different detectives (page 5). What similarities or differences do you notice between Sherlock Holmes and some of the other fictional detectives you know?

## How does Holmes solve the mystery before the reader?

Of course, Holmes solves the mystery first because he is a brilliant detective. But is that the only reason?

**Look at these important clues from 'Silver Blaze'. Each of these clues is revealed bit by bit. Are you given all the information you need to solve the case before Sherlock Holmes reveals the solution? Check Holmes's explanation at the end of the story (pages 25-26) to find out which parts of each clue are not revealed until the end.**

### Clue 1

- Ned Hunter, the stable lad who was drugged, was served curried mutton for supper.
- Only the Strakers could have decided what would be for supper that day.
- Opium has a strong taste so would need to have been given to the stable lad in strong tasting food.

**Holmes deduces: Straker was the person who drugged Hunter.**

### Clue 2

- Straker was holding a knife when he died. It was covered with blood, presumed to be the blood of someone he was fighting.
- He had a cut on his thigh – did he do this himself as he fell?
- The main suspect had no injuries.
- The knife was small, the kind used for delicate medical procedures.
- Several sheep at the stables had gone lame recently.
- You can make a horse go lame by making a tiny cut in the leg tendons.

**Holmes deduces: Straker had practised making sheep go lame. He was then intending to make the horse lame.**

### Clue 3

- The police found a bill in Straker's house. The bill was addressed to 'William Derbyshire'. Mrs Straker said Derbyshire was a friend of her husband's and his post was sometimes sent to their house.
- The bill was for an expensive women's outfit.
- Mrs Straker had never owned a dress like the one on the bill.
- Holmes took a photograph of Straker to the shop that sent the bill. The people in the shop recognised the photo – Straker had been using the name William Derbyshire.

**Holmes deduces: Straker had been using the name William Derbyshire to buy clothes for his mistress. The mistress had expensive taste so Straker needed money. This had led him to try to make the horse go lame so that he could bet against it.**

Reading the stories – Silver Blaze

Notice that in clues 1 and 2, Holmes gets there first because of his brilliance, for example because he has knowledge that the ordinary reader probably doesn't have, such as the fact that opium, the poison, has a strong taste. On the other hand, in clue 3, Conan Doyle cheats a little by keeping back the information Holmes learns from the photograph.

**As you read more Sherlock Holmes stories, look out for the ways Conan Doyle makes sure that Holmes solves the case before the reader.**

## Conan Dolye's style – description

Conan Doyle uses description:
- to set the scene and create atmosphere
- to describe characters
- to give clues.

**Look through the story you have read and find one example of each of these.**

**Now look more closely at the three descriptions on page 29. For each one you are given a re-written version with some descriptive ingredients missing and then the original as written by Conan Doyle. For each example see if you can:**

- decide what ingredients or techniques are missing in the re-written version and label them on the original
- explain the effect of including the techniques – how do they improve the description?

Hint – look for some of the following ingredients:
- metaphors and similes
- interesting vocabulary
- powerful verbs
- alliteration
- variety of sentence length.

**After you have read all three descriptions, write a paragraph about one of these extracts, explaining what descriptive techniques Doyle has used and what effect they might have on the reader.**

**28**    *Studying Sherlock Holmes*      © **English & Media Centre, 2004**

## Describing setting

**The re-written version**

A few minutes later our driver pulled up at a villa. Some distance off, lay an outbuilding. In every other direction you could see the moor as far as the skyline.

**The original**

A few minutes later our driver pulled up at a neat little red-brick villa with overhanging eaves, which stood by the road. Some distance off, across a paddock, lay a long grey-tiled outbuilding. In every other direction the low curves of the moor, bronze-coloured from the fading ferns, stretched away to the skyline, broken only by the steeples of Tavistock, and by a cluster of houses away to the westward which marked the Capelton stables.

## Describing setting and character

**The re-written version**

It was quite twenty minutes, and dusk had turned to night before Holmes and the trainer re-appeared. Never have I seen such a change as was brought about in Silas Brown in that short time. His face was pale, he was sweating, and his hands shook. His bullying, over-bearing manner was all gone too, and he walked along at my companion's side.

**The original**

It was quite twenty minutes, and the reds had all faded into greys before Holmes and the trainer re-appeared. Never have I seen such a change as was brought about in Silas Brown in that short time. His face was ashy pale, beads of perspiration shone upon his brow, and his hands shook until the hunting-crop wagged like a branch in the wind. His bullying, over-bearing manner was all gone too, and he cringed along at my companion's side like a dog with its master.

## Describing the crime scene, giving clues

**The re-written version**

'From that time on all was plain. Straker had led out the horse to a place where his light would be invisible. Simpson had dropped his cravat, and Straker had picked it up – with some idea, perhaps, that he might use it in securing the horse's leg. Once in the hollow, he had got behind the horse and had struck a light; but the creature, frightened at the match, had kicked out, and the horseshoe hit Straker on the forehead. He had already taken off his overcoat in order to do the task, and so, as he fell, his knife cut his thigh. Do I make it clear?'

**The original**

'From that time on all was plain. Straker had led out the horse to a hollow where his light would be invisible. Simpson in his flight had dropped his cravat, and Straker had picked it up – with some idea, perhaps, that he might use it in securing the horse's leg. Once in the hollow, he had got behind the horse and had struck a light; but the creature, frightened at the sudden glare, and with the strange instinct of animals feeling that some mischief was intended, had lashed out, and the steel shoe had struck Straker full on the forehead. He had already, in spite of the rain, taken off his overcoat in order to do his delicate task, and so, as he fell, his knife gashed his thigh. Do I make it clear?'

# A Scandal in Bohemia

## Before reading

### It's a scandal! Looking at the title

Think of possible scandals involving each of the following:

• A celebrity
• Prince William
• The Prime Minister

How many recent scandals can you think of? What seem to be the essential ingredients of a scandal, for example is a lie an essential part of any scandal?

### The opening of the story

Read these three extracts. Which one do you think is the opening of the story? Be prepared to explain the reasons for your choice.

---

**Extract 1**

To Sherlock Holmes she is always *the* woman. I have seldom heard him mention her under any other name. In his eyes she eclipses and predominates the whole of her sex. It was not that he felt any emotion akin to love for Irene Adler.

---

**Extract 2**

I had seen little of Holmes lately. My marriage had drifted us away from each other. My own complete happiness, and the home-centred interests which rise up around the man who first finds himself master of his own establishment, were sufficient to absorb all my attention, while Holmes, who loathed every form of society with his whole Bohemian soul, remained in our lodgings in Baker Street, buried among his old books, and alternating from week to week between cocaine and ambition, the drowsiness of the drug, and the fierce energy of his own keen nature.

---

**Extract 3**

One night – it was on the twentieth of March, 1888 – I was returning from a journey to a patient (for I had now returned to civil practice), when my way led me through Baker Street. As I passed the well-remembered door, which must always be associated in my mind with my wooing, and with the dark incidents of the Study in Scarlet, I was seized with a keen desire to see Holmes again, and to know how he was employing his extraordinary powers. His rooms were brilliantly lit, and, even as I looked up, I saw his tall, spare figure pass twice in a dark silhouette against the blind.

---

## During reading

As you read the story you will find that at each PAUSE symbol there are questions or activities to help you to check your understanding of the story.

# A Scandal in Bohemia

To Sherlock Holmes she is always *the* woman. I have seldom heard him mention her under any other name. In his eyes she eclipses and predominates the whole of her sex. It was not that he felt any emotion akin to love for Irene Adler. All emotions, and that one particularly, were abhorrent to his cold, precise, but admirably balanced mind. He was, I take it, the most perfect reasoning and observing machine that the world has seen: but, as a lover, he would have placed himself in a false position. He never spoke of the softer passions, save with a gibe and a sneer. They were admirable things for the observer – excellent for drawing the veil from men's motives and actions. But for the trained reasoner to admit such intrusions into his own delicate and finely adjusted temperament was to introduce a distracting factor which might throw a doubt upon all his mental results. Grit in a sensitive instrument, or a crack in one of his own high-power lenses, would not be more disturbing than a strong emotion in a nature such as his. And yet there was but one woman to him, and that woman was the late Irene Adler, of dubious and questionable memory.

I had seen little of Holmes lately. My marriage had drifted us away from each other. My own complete happiness, and the home-centred interests which rise up around the man who first finds himself master of his own establishment, were sufficient to absorb all my attention; while Holmes, who loathed every form of society with his whole Bohemian soul, remained in our lodgings in Baker Street, buried among his old books, and alternating from week to week between cocaine and ambition, the drowsiness of the drug, and the fierce energy of his own keen nature. He was still, as ever, deeply attracted by the study of crime, and occupied his immense faculties and extraordinary powers of observation in following out those clues, and clearing up those mysteries which had been abandoned as hopeless by the official police. From time to time I heard some vague account of his doings: of his summons to Odessa in the case of the Trepoff murder, of his clearing up of the singular tragedy of the Atkinson brothers, at Trincomalee, and finally of the mission which he had accomplished so delicately and successfully for the reigning family of Holland. Beyond these signs of his activity, however, which I merely shared with all the readers of the daily press, I knew little of my former friend and companion.

One night – it was on the twentieth of March, 1888 – I was returning from a journey to a patient (for I had now returned to civil practice), when my way led me through Baker Street. As I passed the well-remembered door, which must always be associated in my mind with my wooing, and with the dark incidents of the Study in Scarlet, I was seized with a keen desire to see Holmes again, and to know how he was employing his extraordinary powers. His rooms were brilliantly lit, and, even as I looked up, I saw his tall, spare figure pass twice in a dark silhouette against the blind. He was pacing the room swiftly, eagerly, with his head sunk upon his chest, and his hands clasped behind him. To me, who knew his every mood and habit, his attitude and manner told their own story. He was at work again. He had risen out of his drug-created dreams and was hot upon the scent of some new problem. I rang the bell, and was shown up to the chamber which had formerly been in part my own.

---

**PAUSE**    **Now discuss the questions listed here.**

---

- Was the opening paragraph the one you chose? Does Doyle's choice surprise you?
- Why do you think Conan Doyle chose to start the story in this way? How does the first paragraph make you want to read the rest of the story?

Some historical information, which may help you to understand the story is given below.

- The theatre and the opera were not considered to be particularly respectable places to work, especially for women. A woman working in one of these professions would be considered, perhaps, as a Page Three girl might be considered now.
- Royalty had more importance, power and influence than today.

His manner was not effusive. It seldom was; but he was glad, I think, to see me. With hardly a word spoken, but with a kindly eye, he waved me to an armchair, threw across his case of cigars, and indicated a spirit case and a gasogene in the corner. Then he stood before the fire, and looked me over in his singular introspective fashion.

'Wedlock suits you,' he remarked. 'I think, Watson, that you have put on seven and a half pounds since I saw you.

'Seven,' I answered.

'Indeed, I should have thought a little more. Just a trifle more, I fancy, Watson. And in practice again, I observe. You did not tell me that you intended to go into harness.'

'Then, how do you know?'

'I see it, I deduce it. How do I know that you have been getting yourself very wet lately, and that you have a most clumsy and careless servant girl?'

'My dear Holmes,' said I, 'this is too much. You would certainly have been burned had you lived a few centuries ago. It is true that I had a country walk on Thursday and came home in a dreadful mess; but as I have changed my clothes I can't imagine how you deduce it. As to Mary Jane, she is incorrigible, and my wife has given her notice; but there, again, I fail to see how you work it out.'

He chuckled to himself and rubbed his long, nervous hands together.

'It is simplicity itself,' said he; 'my eyes tell me that on the inside of your left shoe, just where the firelight strikes it, the leather is scored by six almost parallel cuts. Obviously they have been caused by someone who has very carelessly scraped round the edges of the sole in order to remove crusted mud from it. Hence, you see, my double deduction that you had been out in vile weather, and that you had a particularly malignant boot-slitting specimen of the London slavey. As to your practice, if a gentleman walks into my rooms smelling of iodoform, with a black mark of nitrate of silver upon his right forefinger, and a bulge on the right side of his top-hat to show where he has secreted his stethoscope, I must be dull, indeed, if I do not pronounce him to be an active member of the medical profession.'

I could not help laughing at the ease with which he explained his process of deduction. 'When I hear you give your reasons,' I remarked, 'the thing always appears to me to be so ridiculously simple that I could easily do it myself, though at each successive instance of your reasoning I am baffled until you explain your process. And yet I believe that my eyes are as good as yours.'

'Quite so,' he answered, lighting a cigarette, and throwing himself down into an armchair. 'You see, but you do not observe. The distinction is clear. For example, you have frequently seen the steps which lead up from the hall to this room.'

'Frequently.'

'How often?'

'Well, some hundreds of times.'

'Then how many are there?'

'How many! I don't know.'

'Quite so! You have not observed. And yet you have seen. That is just my point. Now, I know that there are seventeen steps, because I have both seen and observed. By the way, since you are interested in these little problems, and since you are good enough to chronicle one or two of my trifling experiences, you may be interested in this.' He threw over a sheet of thick, pink-tinted note-paper which had been lying open upon the table. 'It came by the last post,' said he. 'Read it aloud.'

**PAUSE**      **Discuss what you have learned from the story so far about Holmes's methods of detection. Make some notes as these will help you later – if you have read 'Silver Blaze', you could add to the notes you made on that story.**

The note was undated, and without either signature or address.

'There will call upon you tonight, at a quarter to eight o'clock [it said], a gentleman who desires to consult you upon a matter of the very deepest moment. Your recent services to one of the royal houses of Europe have shown that you are one who may safely be trusted with matters which are of an importance which can hardly be exaggerated. This account of you we have from all quarters received. Be in your chamber then at that hour, and do not take it amiss if your visitor wear a mask.'

'This is indeed a mystery,' I remarked. 'What do you imagine that it means?'

'I have no data yet. It is a capital mistake to theorize before one has data. Insensibly one begins to twist facts to suit theories, instead of theories to suit facts. But the note itself. What do you deduce from it?'

I carefully examined the writing, and the paper upon which it was written.

'The man who wrote it was presumably well-to-do,' I remarked, endeavouring to imitate my companion's processes. 'Such paper could not be bought under half a crown a packet. It is peculiarly strong and stiff.'

'Peculiar – that is the very word,' said Holmes. 'It is not an English paper at all. Hold it up to the light.'

I did so, and saw a large E with a small g, a P, and a large G with a small t woven into the texture of the paper.

'What do you make of that?' asked Holmes.

'The name of the maker, no doubt; or his monogram, rather.'

'Not at all. The G with the small t stands for 'Gesellschaft,' which is the German for 'Company.' It is a customary contraction like our 'Co.' P, of course, stands for 'Papier.' Now for the Eg. Let us glance at our Continental Gazetteer.' He took down a heavy brown volume from his shelves. 'Eglow, Eglonitz – here we are, Egria. It is in a German-speaking country – in Bohemia, not far from Carlsbad. 'Remarkable as being the scene of the death of Wallenstein, and for its numerous glass factories and paper mills.' Ha, ha, my boy, what do you make of that?' His eyes sparkled, and he sent up a great blue triumphant cloud from his cigarette.

'The paper was made in Bohemia,' I said.

'Precisely. And the man who wrote the note is a German. Do you note the peculiar construction of the sentence – 'This account of you we have from all quarters received.' A Frenchman or Russian could not have written that. It is the German who is so uncourteous to his verbs. It only remains, therefore, to discover what is wanted by this German who writes upon Bohemian paper and prefers wearing a mask to showing his face. And here he comes, if I am not mistaken, to resolve all our doubts.'

As he spoke there was the sharp sound of horses' hoofs and grating wheels against the curb, followed by a sharp pull at the bell. Holmes whistled.

'A pair by the sound,' said he. 'Yes,' he continued, glancing out of the window. 'A nice little brougham and a pair of beauties. A hundred and fifty guineas apiece. There's money in this case, Watson, if there is nothing else.'

'I think that I had better go, Holmes.'

'Not a bit, Doctor. Stay where you are. I am lost without my Boswell*. And this promises to be interesting. It would be a pity to miss it.'

'But your client –'

'Never mind him. I may want your help, and so may he. Here he comes. Sit down in that armchair, Doctor, and give us your best attention.'

A slow and heavy step, which had been heard upon the stairs and in the passage, paused immediately outside the door. Then there was a loud and authoritative tap.

'Come in!' said Holmes.

A man entered who could hardly have been less than six feet six inches in height, with the chest and limbs of a Hercules. His dress was rich with a richness which would, in England, be looked upon as akin to bad taste. Heavy bands of astrakhan were slashed across the sleeves and fronts of his double-breasted coat, while the deep blue cloak which was thrown over his shoulders was lined with flame-coloured silk and secured at the neck with a brooch which consisted of a single flaming beryl. Boots which extended halfway up his calves, and which were trimmed at the tops with rich brown fur, completed the impression of barbaric opulence which was suggested by his whole appearance. He carried a broad-brimmed hat in his hand, while he wore across the upper part of his face, extending down past the cheekbones, a black vizard mask, which he had apparently adjusted that very moment, for his hand was still raised to it as he entered. From the lower part of the face he appeared to be a man of strong character, with a thick, hanging lip, and a long, straight chin suggestive of resolution pushed to the length of obstinacy.

'You had my note?' he asked with a deep harsh voice and a strongly marked German accent. 'I told you that I would call.' He looked from one to the other of us, as if uncertain which to address.

* Boswell was a famous biographer of Samuel Johnson

'Pray take a seat,' said Holmes. This is my friend and colleague, Dr Watson, who is occasionally good enough to help me in my cases. Whom have I the honour to address?'

'You may address me as the Count von Kramm, a Bohemian nobleman. I understand that this gentleman, your friend, is a man of honour and discretion, whom I may trust with a matter of the most extreme importance. If not, I should much prefer to communicate with you alone.'

I rose to go, but Holmes caught me by the wrist and pushed me back into my chair. 'It is both, or none,' said he. 'You may say before this gentleman anything which you may say to me.'

The Count shrugged his broad shoulders. 'Then I must begin,' said he, 'by binding you both to absolute secrecy for two years; at the end of that time the matter will be of no importance. At present it is not too much to say that it is of such weight it may have an influence upon European history.'

'I promise,' said Holmes.

'And I.'

'You will excuse this mask,' continued our strange visitor. 'The august person who employs me wishes his agent to be unknown to you, and I may confess at once that the title by which I have just called myself is not exactly my own.'

'I was aware of it,' said Holmes dryly.

'The circumstances are of great delicacy, and every precaution has to be taken to quench what might grow to be an immense scandal and seriously compromise one of the reigning families of Europe. To speak plainly, the matter implicates the great House of Ormstein, hereditary kings of Bohemia.'

'I was also aware of that,' murmured Holmes, settling himself down in his arm-chair, and closing his eyes.

Our visitor glanced with some apparent surprise at the languid, lounging figure of the man who had been, no doubt, depicted to him as the most incisive reasoner, and most energetic agent in Europe. Holmes slowly reopened his eyes and looked impatiently at his gigantic client.

**PAUSE**   **If you were the client, what would be your first impressions of Holmes? Discuss your ideas with a partner.**

'If your Majesty would condescend to state your case,' he remarked, 'I should be better able to advise you.'

The man sprang from his chair, and paced up and down the room in uncontrollable agitation. Then, with a gesture of desperation, he tore the mask from his face and hurled it upon the ground.

'You are right,' he cried; 'I am the King. Why should I attempt to conceal it?'

'Why, indeed?' murmured Holmes. 'Your Majesty had not spoken before I was aware that I was addressing Wilhelm Gottsreich Sigismond von Ormstein, Grand Duke of Cassel-Felstein, and hereditary King of Bohemia.'

'But you can understand,' said our strange visitor, sitting down once more and passing his hand over his high white forehead, 'you can understand that I am not accustomed to doing such business in my own person. Yet the matter was so delicate that I could not confide it to an agent without putting myself in his power. I have come *incognito* from Prague for the purpose of consulting you.'

'Then, pray consult,' said Holmes, shutting his eyes once more.

'The facts are briefly these: some five years ago, during a lengthy visit to Warsaw, I made the acquaintance of the well-known adventuress, Irene Adler. The name is no doubt familiar to you.'

'Kindly look her up in my index, Doctor,' murmured Holmes without opening his eyes. For many years he had adopted a system of docketing all paragraphs concerning men and things, so that it was difficult to name a subject or a person on which he could not at once furnish information. In this case I found her biography sandwiched in between that of a Hebrew rabbi and that of a staff-commander who had written a monograph upon the deep-sea fishes.

'Let me see,' said Holmes. 'Hum! Born in New Jersey in the year 1858. Contralto – hum! La Scala, hum! Prima Donna Imperial Opera of Warsaw – yes! Retired from operatic stage – ha! Living in London – quite so! Your Majesty, as I understand, became entangled with this young person, wrote her some compromising letters, and is now desirous of getting those letters back.'

'Precisely so. But how –'

'Was there a secret marriage?'

'None.'

'No legal papers or certificates?'

'None.'

'Then I fail to follow Your Majesty. If this young person should produce her letters for blackmailing or other purposes, how is she to prove their authenticity?'

'There is the writing.'

'Pooh, pooh! Forgery.'

'My private note-paper.'

'Stolen.'

'My own seal.'

'Imitated.'

'My photograph.'

'Bought.'

'We were both in the photograph.'

'Oh, dear! That is very bad! Your Majesty has indeed committed an indiscretion.'

'I was mad – insane.'

'You have compromised yourself seriously.'

'I was only Crown Prince then. I was young. I am but thirty now.'

'It must be recovered.'

'We have tried and failed.'

'Your Majesty must pay. It must be bought.'

'She will not sell.'

'Stolen, then.'

'Five attempts have been made. Twice burglars in my pay ransacked her house. Once we diverted her luggage when she travelled. Twice she has been waylaid. There has been no result.'

'No sign of it?'

'Absolutely none.'

Holmes laughed. 'It is quite a pretty little problem,' said he.

'But a very serious one to me,' returned the King reproachfully.

'Very, indeed. And what does she propose to do with the photograph?'

'To ruin me.'

'But how?'

'I am about to be married.'

'So I have heard.'

'To Clotilde Lothman von Saxe-Meningen, second daughter of the King of Scandinavia. You may know the strict principles of her family. She is herself the very soul of delicacy. A shadow of a doubt as to my conduct would bring the matter to an end.'

'And Irene Adler?'

'Threatens to send them the photograph. And she will do it. I know that she will do it. You do not know her, but she has a soul of steel. She has the face of the most beautiful of women, and the mind of the most resolute of men. Rather than I should marry another woman, there are no lengths to which she would not go – none.'

'You are sure that she has not sent it yet?'

'I am sure.'

'And why?'

'Because she has said that she would send it on the day when the betrothal was publicly proclaimed. That will be next Monday.'

'Oh, then, we have three days yet,' said Holmes with a yawn. 'That is very fortunate, as I have one or two matters of importance to look into just at present. Your Majesty will, of course, stay in London for the present?'

'Certainly. You will find me at the Langham under the name of the Count von Kramm.'

'Then I shall drop you a line to let you know how we progress.'

'Pray do so. I shall be all anxiety.'

'Then, as to money?'

'You have *carte blanche.*'

'Absolutely?'

'I tell you that I would give one of the provinces of my kingdom to have that photograph.'

'And for present expenses?'

The King took a heavy chamois leather bag from under his cloak and laid it on the table.

'There are three hundred pounds in gold and seven hundred in notes,' he said.

Holmes scribbled a receipt upon a sheet of his note-book, and handed it to him.

'And mademoiselle's address?' he asked.

'Is Bryony Lodge, Serpentine Avenue, St. John's Wood.'

Holmes took a note of it. 'One other question,' said he. 'Was the photograph a cabinet?'*

'It was.'

'Then, good night, Your Majesty, and I trust that we shall soon have some good news for you. And good night, Watson,' he added, as the wheels of the royal brougham rolled down the street. 'If you will be good enough to call tomorrow afternoon at three o'clock I should like to chat this little matter over with you.'

*\* A size of photograph, designed to be displayed in a cabinet*

**PAUSE**      **Discuss what you learn about Holmes from the way he treats the King.**

At three o'clock precisely I was at Baker Street, but Holmes had not yet returned. The landlady informed me that he had left the house shortly after eight o'clock in the morning. I sat down beside the fire, however, with the intention of awaiting him, however long he might be. I was already deeply interested in his inquiry, for, though it was surrounded by none of the grim and strange features which were associated with the two crimes which I have already recorded, still, the nature of the case and the exalted station of his client gave it a character of its own. Indeed, apart from the nature of the investigation which my friend had on hand, there was something in his masterly grasp of a situation, and his keen, incisive reasoning, which made it a pleasure to me to study his system of work, and to follow the quick, subtle methods by which he disentangled the most inextricable mysteries. So accustomed was I to his invariable success that the very possibility of his failing had ceased to enter into my head.

It was close upon four before the door opened, and a drunken-looking groom, ill-kempt and side-whiskered with an inflamed face and disreputable clothes, walked into the room.

Accustomed as I was to my friend's amazing powers in the use of disguises, I had to look three times before I was certain that it was indeed he. With a nod he vanished into the bedroom, whence he emerged in five minutes tweed-suited and respectable, as of old. Putting his hands into his pockets, he stretched out his legs in front of the fire and laughed heartily for some minutes.

'Well, really!' he cried, and then he choked; and laughed again until he was obliged to lie back, limp and helpless, in the chair.

'What is it?'

'It's quite too funny. I am sure you could never guess how I employed my morning, or what I ended by doing.'

'I can't imagine. I suppose that you have been watching the habits, and perhaps the house, of Miss Irene Adler.'

'Quite so; but the sequel was rather unusual. I will tell you, however. I left the house a little after eight o'clock this morning in the character of a groom out of work. There is a wonderful sympathy and freemasonry among horsey men. Be one of them, and you will know all that there is to know. I soon found Briony Lodge. It is a bijou villa, with a garden at the back, but built out in front right up to the road, two stories. Chubb lock to the door. Large sitting-room on the right side, well furnished, with long windows almost to the floor, and those preposterous English window fasteners which a child could open. Behind there was nothing remarkable, save that the passage window could be reached from the top of the coach-house. I walked round it and examined it closely from every point of view, but without noting anything else of interest.

'I then lounged down the street, and found, as I expected, that there was a mews in a lane which runs down by one wall of the garden. I lent the ostlers a hand in rubbing down their horses, and received in exchange twopence, a glass of half and half, two fills of shag tobacco, and as much information as I could desire about Miss Adler, to say nothing of half a dozen other people in the neighbourhood in whom I was not in the least interested, but whose biographies I was compelled to listen to.'

'And what of Irene Adler?' I asked.

'Oh, she has turned all the men's heads down in that part. She is the daintiest thing under a bonnet on this planet. So say the Serpentine Mews, to a man. She lives quietly, sings at concerts, drives out at five every day, and returns at seven sharp for dinner. Seldom goes out at other times, except when she sings. Has only one male visitor, but a good deal of him. He is dark, handsome, and dashing, never calls less than once a day, and often twice. He is a Mr Godfrey Norton, of the Inner Temple. See the advantages of a cabman as a confidant. They had driven him home a dozen times from Serpentine-mews, and knew all about him. When I had listened to all they had to tell, I began to walk up and down near Briony Lodge once more, and to think over my plan of campaign.

'This Godfrey Norton was evidently an important factor in the matter. He was a lawyer. That sounded ominous. What was the relation between them, and what the object of his repeated visits? Was she his client, his friend, or his mistress? If the former, she had probably transferred the photograph to his keeping. If the latter, it was less likely. On the issue of this question depended whether I should continue my work at Briony Lodge, or turn my attention to the gentleman's chambers in the Temple. It was a delicate point, and it widened the field of my inquiry. I fear that I bore you with these details, but I have to let you see my little difficulties, if you are to understand the situation.'

'I am following you closely,' I answered.

'I was still balancing the matter in my mind when a hansom cab drove up to Briony Lodge, and a gentleman sprang out. He was a remarkably handsome man, dark, aquiline, and moustached – evidently the man of whom I had heard. He appeared to be in a great hurry, shouted to the cabman to wait, and brushed past the maid who opened the door with the air of a man who was thoroughly at home.

'He was in the house about half an hour, and I could catch glimpses of him, in the windows of the sitting-room, pacing up and down, talking excitedly, and waving his arms. Of her I could see nothing. Presently he emerged, looking even more flurried than before. As he stepped up to the cab, he pulled a gold watch from his pocket and looked at it earnestly. "Drive like the devil," he shouted, "first to Gross & Hankey's in Regent Street, and then to the Church of St. Monica in the Edgeware Road. Half a guinea if you do it in twenty minutes!"

'Away they went, and I was just wondering whether I should not do well to follow them when up the lane came a neat little landau, the coachman with his coat only half-buttoned, and his tie under his ear, while all the tags of his harness were sticking out of the buckles. It hadn't pulled up before she shot out of the hall door and into it. I only caught a glimpse of her at the moment, but she was a lovely woman, with a face that a man might die for.

'"The Church of St. Monica, John," she cried, "and half a sovereign if you reach it in twenty minutes."

'This was quite too good to lose, Watson. I was just balancing whether I should run for it, or whether I should perch behind her landau when a cab came through the street. The driver looked twice at such a shabby fare, but I jumped in before he could object. "The Church of St. Monica," said I, "and half a sovereign if you reach it in twenty minutes." It was twenty-five minutes to twelve, and of course it was clear enough what was in the wind.*

'My cabby drove fast. I don't think I ever drove faster, but the others were there before us. The cab and the landau with their steaming horses were in front of the door when I arrived. I paid the man and hurried into the church. There was not a soul there save the two whom I had followed, and a surpliced clergyman, who seemed to be expostulating with them. They were all three standing in a knot in front of the altar. I lounged up the side aisle like any other idler who has dropped into a church. Suddenly, to my surprise, the three at the altar faced round to me, and Godfrey Norton came running as hard as he could towards me.

'"Thank God!" he cried. "You'll do. Come! Come!"

'"What then?" I asked.

'"Come, man, come, only three minutes, or it won't be legal."

'I was half-dragged up to the altar, and before I knew where I was, I found myself mumbling responses which were whispered in my ear, and vouching for things of which I knew nothing, and generally assisting in the secure tying up of Irene Adler, spinster, to Godfrey Norton, bachelor. It was all done in an instant, and there was the gentleman thanking me on the one side and the lady on the other, while the clergyman beamed on me in front.

*Until 1886, marriages could be legally performed only between 8am and 12 noon*

It was the most preposterous position in which I ever found myself in my life, and it was the thought of it that started me laughing just now. It seems that there had been some informality about their licence, that the clergyman absolutely refused to marry them without a witness of some sort, and that my lucky appearance saved the bridegroom from having to sally out into the streets in search of a best man. The bride gave me a sovereign, and I mean to wear it on my watch-chain in memory of the occasion.'

'This is a very unexpected turn of affairs,' said I; 'and what then?'

'Well, I found my plans very seriously menaced. It looked as if the pair might take an immediate departure, and so necessitate very prompt and energetic measures on my part. At the church door, however, they separated, he driving back to the Temple, and she to her own house. '"I shall drive out in the park at five as usual," she said as she left him. I heard no more. They drove away in different directions, and I went off to make my own arrangements.'

'Which are?'

'Some cold beef and a glass of beer,' he answered, ringing the bell. 'I have been too busy to think of food, and I am likely to be busier still this evening. By the way, Doctor, I shall want your co-operation.'

'I shall be delighted.'

'You don't mind breaking the law?'

'Not in the least.'

'Nor running a chance of arrest?'

'Not in a good cause.'

'Oh, the cause is excellent!'

'Then I am your man.'

'I was sure that I might rely on you.'

'But what is it you wish?'

'When Mrs Turner has brought in the tray I will make it clear to you. Now,' he said as he turned hungrily on the simple fare that our landlady had provided, 'I must discuss it while I eat, for I have not much time. It is nearly five now. In two hours we must be on the scene of action. Miss Irene, or Madame, rather, returns from her drive at seven. We must be at Briony Lodge to meet her.'

'And what then?'

'You must leave that to me. I have already arranged what is to occur. There is only one point on which I must insist. You must not interfere, come what may. You understand?'

'I am to be neutral?'

'To do nothing whatever. There will probably be some small unpleasantness. Do not join in it. It will end in my being conveyed into the house. Four or five minutes afterwards the sitting-room window will open. You are to station yourself close to that open window.'

'Yes.'

'You are to watch me, for I will be visible to you.'

'Yes.'

'And when I raise my hand – so – you will throw into the room what I give you to throw, and will, at the same time, raise the cry of fire. You quite follow me?'

'Entirely.'

'It is nothing very formidable,' he said, taking a long cigar-shaped roll from his pocket. 'It is an ordinary plumber's smoke rocket, fitted with a cap at either end to make it self-lighting. Your task is confined to that. When you raise your cry of fire, it will be taken up by quite a number of people. You may then walk to the end of the street, and I will rejoin you in ten minutes. I hope that I have made myself clear?'

'I am to remain neutral, to get near the window, to watch you, and, at the signal, to throw in this object, then to raise the cry of fire, and to await you at the corner of the street.'

'Precisely.'

'Then you may entirely rely on me.'

'That is excellent. I think, perhaps, it is almost time that I prepare for the new role I have to play.'

He disappeared into his bedroom, and returned in a few minutes in the character of an amiable and simple-minded Non-conformist clergyman. His broad black hat, his baggy trousers, his white tie, his sympathetic smile, and general look of peering and benevolent curiosity were such as Mr John Hare alone could have equalled. It was not merely that Holmes changed his costume. His expression, his manner, his very soul seemed to vary with every fresh part that he assumed. The stage lost a fine actor, even as science lost an acute reasoner, when he became a specialist in crime.

**PAUSE**     **Discuss what you learn about Watson from the way he responds to Holmes's requests. Consider the questions below.**

- What kind of person is Watson?
- Why is he a good assistant for Holmes?

It was a quarter past six when we left Baker Street, and it still wanted ten minutes to the hour when we found ourselves in Serpentine Avenue. It was already dusk, and the lamps were just being lighted as we paced up and down in front of Briony Lodge, waiting for the coming of its occupant. The house was just such as I had pictured it from Sherlock Holmes's succinct description, but the locality appeared to be less private than I expected. On the contrary, for a small street in a quiet neighbourhood, it was remarkably animated. There was a group of shabbily dressed men smoking and laughing in a corner, a scissors-grinder with his wheel, two guardsmen who were flirting with a nurse-girl, and several well-dressed young men who were lounging up and down with cigars in their mouths.

'You see,' remarked Holmes, as we paced to and fro in front of the house, 'this marriage rather simplifies matters. The photograph becomes a double-edged weapon now. The chances are that she would be as averse to its being seen by Mr Godfrey Norton, as our client is to its coming to the eyes of his Princess. Now the question is – Where are we to find the photograph?'

'Where, indeed?'

'It is most unlikely that she carries it about with her. It is cabinet size. Too large for easy concealment about a woman's dress. She knows that the King is capable of having her waylaid and searched. Two attempts of the sort have already been made. We may take it, then, that she does not carry it about with her.'

'Where, then?'

'Her banker or her lawyer. There is that double possibility. But I am inclined to think neither. Women are naturally secretive, and they like to do their own secreting. Why should she hand it over to anyone else? She could trust her own guardianship, but she could not tell what indirect or political influence might be brought to bear upon a businessman. Besides, remember that she had resolved to use it within a few days. It must be where she can lay her hands upon it. It must be in her own house.'

'But it has twice been burgled.'

'Pshaw! They did not know how to look.'

'But how will you look?'

'I will not look.'

'What then?'

'I will get her to show me.'

'But she will refuse.'

'She will not be able to. But I hear the rumble of wheels. It is her carriage. Now carry out my orders to the letter.'

**PAUSE**     **As a class, brainstorm any theories you have about how Holmes is going to get Irene Adler to 'show him' where she has hidden the photograph.**

As he spoke the gleam of the sidelights of a carriage came round the curve of the avenue. It was a smart little landau which rattled up to the door of Briony Lodge. As it pulled up, one of the loafing men at the corner dashed forward to open the door in the hope of earning a copper, but was elbowed away by another loafer, who had rushed up with the same intention. A fierce quarrel broke out, which was increased by the two guardsmen, who took sides with one of the loungers, and by the scissors-grinder, who was equally hot upon the other side. A blow was struck, and in an instant the lady, who had stepped from her carriage, was the centre of a little knot of flushed and struggling men, who struck savagely at each other with their fists and sticks. Holmes dashed into the crowd to protect the lady; but just as he reached her he gave a cry and dropped to the ground, with the blood running freely down his face. At his fall the guardsmen took to their heels in one direction and the loungers in the other, while a number of better dressed people, who had watched the scuffle without taking part in it, crowded in to help the lady and to attend to the injured man. Irene Adler, as I will still call her, had hurried up the steps; but she stood at the top with her superb figure outlined against the lights of the hall, looking back into the street.

'Is the poor gentleman much hurt?' she asked.

'He is dead,' cried several voices.

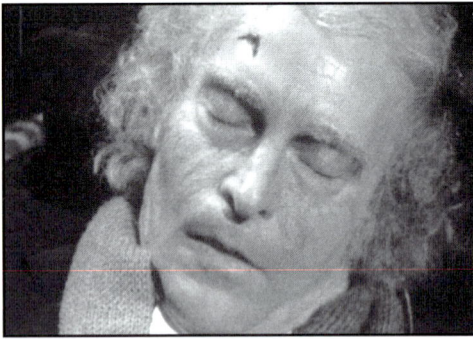

'No, no, there's life in him!' shouted another. 'But he'll be gone before you can get him to hospital.'

'He's a brave fellow,' said a woman. 'They would have had the lady's purse and watch if it hadn't been for him. They were a gang, and a rough one, too. Ah, he's breathing now.'

'He can't lie in the street. May we bring him in, marm?'

'Surely. Bring him into the sitting-room. There is a comfortable sofa. This way, please!'

Slowly and solemnly he was borne into Briony Lodge and laid out in the principal room, while I still observed the proceedings from my post by the window. The lamps had been lit, but the blinds had not been drawn, so that I could see Holmes as he lay upon the couch. I do not know whether he was seized with compunction at that moment for the part he was playing, but I know that I never felt more heartily ashamed of myself in my life than when I saw the beautiful creature against whom I was conspiring, or the grace and kindliness with which she waited upon the injured man. And yet it would be the blackest treachery to Holmes to draw back now from the part which he had entrusted to me. I hardened my heart, and took the smoke-rocket from under my ulster. After all, I thought, we are not injuring her. We are but preventing her from injuring another.

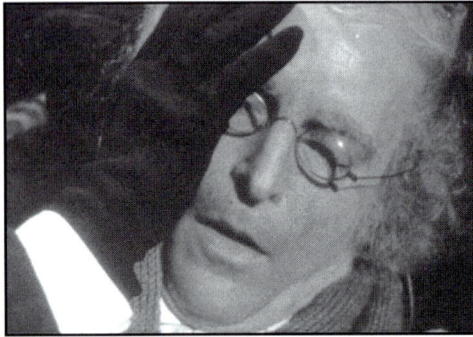

Holmes had sat up upon the couch, and I saw him motion like a man who is in need of air. A maid rushed across and threw open the window. At the same instant I saw him raise his hand, and at the signal I tossed my rocket into the room with a cry of 'Fire!' The word was no sooner out of my mouth than the whole crowd of spectators, well dressed and ill – gentlemen, ostlers, and servant-maids – joined in a general shriek of 'Fire!' Thick clouds of smoke curled through the room and out at the open window. I caught a glimpse of rushing figures, and a moment later the voice of Holmes from within assuring them that it was a false alarm. Slipping through the shouting crowd I made my way to the corner of the street, and in ten minutes was rejoiced to find my friend's arm in mine, and to get away from the scene of uproar. He walked swiftly and in silence for some few minutes until we had turned down one of the quiet streets which lead towards the Edgeware Road.

'You did it very nicely, Doctor,' he remarked. 'Nothing could have been better. It is all right.'

'You have the photograph?'

'I know where it is.'

'And how did you find out?'

'She showed me, as I told you she would.'

'I am still in the dark.'

'I do not wish to make a mystery,' said he, laughing. 'The matter was perfectly simple. You, of course, saw that everyone in the street was an accomplice. They were all engaged for the evening.'

'I guessed as much.'

'Then, when the row broke out, I had a little moist red paint in the palm of my hand. I rushed forward, fell down, clapped my hand to my face, and became a piteous spectacle. It is an old trick.'

'That also I could fathom.'

'Then they carried me in. She was bound to have me in. What else could she do? And into her sitting-room, which was the very room which I suspected. It lay between that and her bedroom, and I was determined to see which. They laid me on a couch, I motioned for air, they were compelled to open the window, and you had your chance.'

'How did that help you?'

'It was all-important. When a woman thinks that her house is on fire, her instinct is at once to rush to the thing which she values most. It is a perfectly overpowering impulse, and I have more than once taken advantage of it. In the case of the Darlington substitution scandal it was of use to me, and also in the Arnsworth Castle business. A married woman grabs at her baby – an unmarried one reaches for her jewel box. Now it was clear to me that our lady of today had nothing in the house more precious to her than what we are in quest of. She would rush to secure it. The alarm of fire was admirably done. The smoke and shouting were enough to shake nerves of steel. She responded beautifully. The photograph is in a recess behind a sliding panel just above the right bell-pull. She was there in an instant, and I caught a glimpse of it as she half-drew it out. When I cried out that it was a false alarm, she replaced it, glanced at the rocket, rushed from the room, and I have not seen her since. I rose, and, making my excuses, escaped from the house. I hesitated whether to attempt to secure the photograph at once; but the coachman had come in, and as he was watching me narrowly it seemed safer to wait. A little over-precipitance may ruin all.'

'And now?' I asked.

'Our quest is practically finished. I shall call with the King tomorrow, and with you, if you care to come with us. We will be shown into the sitting-room to wait for the lady; but it is probable that when she comes she may find neither us nor the photograph. It might be a satisfaction to His Majesty to regain it with his own hands.'

'And when will you call?'

'At eight in the morning. She will not be up, so that we shall have a clear field. Besides, we must be prompt, for this marriage may mean a complete change in her life and habits. I must wire to the King without delay.'

We had reached Baker Street and had stopped at the door. He was searching his pockets for the key, when someone passing said:

'Good night, Mister Sherlock Holmes.'

There were several people on the pavement at the time, but the greeting appeared to come from a slim youth in an ulster who had hurried by.

'I've heard that voice before,' said Holmes, staring down the dimly lit street. 'Now, I wonder who the deuce that could have been.'

I slept at Baker Street that night, and we were engaged upon our toast and coffee in the morning when the King of Bohemia rushed into the room.

'You have really got it!' he cried, grasping Sherlock Holmes by either shoulder, and looking eagerly into his face.

'Not yet.'

'But you have hopes?'

'I have hopes.'

'Then, come. I am all impatience to be gone.'

'We must have a cab.'

'No, my brougham is waiting.'

'Then that will simplify matters.'

We descended and started off once more for Briony Lodge.

'Irene Adler is married,' remarked Holmes.

'Married! When?'

'Yesterday.'

'But to whom?

'To an English lawyer named Norton.'

'But she could not love him.'

'I am in hopes that she does.'

'And why in hopes?'

'Because it would spare Your Majesty all fear of future annoyance. If the lady loves her husband, she does not love Your Majesty. If she does not love Your Majesty, there is no reason why she should interfere with Your Majesty's plan.'

'It is true. And yet –! Well! I wish she had been of my own station! What a queen she would have made!' He relapsed into a moody silence which was not broken until we drew up in Serpentine Avenue.

The door of Briony Lodge was open, and an elderly woman stood upon the steps. She watched us with a sardonic eye as we stepped from the brougham.

'Mr Sherlock Holmes, I believe?' said she.

'I am Mr Holmes,' answered my companion, looking at her with a questioning and rather startled gaze.

'Indeed! My mistress told me that you were likely to call. She left this morning with her husband by the 5:15 train from Charing Cross for the Continent.'

'What!' Sherlock Holmes staggered back, white with chagrin and surprise. 'Do you mean that she has left England?'

'Never to return.'

'And the papers?' asked the King hoarsely. 'All is lost.'

'We shall see.' He pushed past the servant, and rushed into the drawing-room, followed by the King and myself. The furniture was scattered about in every direction, with dismantled shelves, and open drawers, as if the lady had hurriedly ransacked them before her flight. Holmes rushed at the bell-pull, tore back a small sliding shutter, and, plunging in his hand, pulled out a photograph and a letter. The photograph was of Irene Adler herself in evening dress, the letter was superscribed to 'Sherlock Holmes, Esq. To be left till called for.' My friend tore it open and we all three read it together. It was dated at midnight of the preceding night and ran in this way:

---

MY DEAR MR SHERLOCK HOLMES:

You really did it very well. You took me in completely. Until after the alarm of fire, I had not a suspicion. But then, when I found how I had betrayed myself, I began to think. I had been warned against you months ago. I had been told that if the King employed an agent it would certainly be you. And your address had been given me. Yet, with all this, you made me reveal what you wanted to know. Even after I became suspicious, I found it hard to think evil of such a dear, kind old clergyman. But, you know, I have been trained as an actress myself. Male costume is nothing new to me. I often take advantage of the freedom which it gives. I sent John, the coachman, to watch you, ran upstairs, got into my walking-clothes, as I call them, and came down just as you departed.

Well, I followed you to your door, and so made sure that I was really an object of interest to the celebrated Mr Sherlock Holmes. Then I, rather imprudently, wished you good night, and started for the Temple to see my husband.

We both thought the best resource was flight, when pursued by so formidable an antagonist; so you will find the nest empty when you call tomorrow. As to the photograph, your client may rest in peace. I love and am loved by a better man than he. The King may do what he will without hindrance from one whom he has cruelly wronged. I keep it only to safeguard myself, and to preserve a weapon which will always secure me from any steps which he might take in the future. I leave a photograph which he might care to possess; and I remain, dear Mr Sherlock Holmes, very truly yours,

Irene Norton, née ADLER.

---

'What a woman – oh, what a woman!' cried the King of Bohemia, when we had all three read this epistle. 'Did I not tell you how quick and resolute she was? Would she not have made an admirable queen? Is it not a pity that she was not on my level?'

'From what I have seen of the lady, she seems, indeed to be on a very different level to your Majesty,' said Holmes coldly. 'I am sorry that I have not been able to bring Your Majesty's business to a more successful conclusion.'

'On the contrary, my dear sir,' cried the King. 'Nothing could be more successful. I know that her word is inviolate. The photograph is now as safe as if it were in the fire.'

'I am glad to hear Your Majesty say so.'

'I am immensely indebted to you. Pray tell me in what way I can reward you. This ring –' He slipped an emerald snake ring from his finger and held it out upon the palm of his hand.

'Your Majesty has something which I should value even more highly,' said Holmes.

'You have but to name it.'

'This photograph!'

The King stared at him in amazement.

'Irene's photograph!' he cried. 'Certainly, if you wish it.'

'I thank Your Majesty. Then there is no more to be done in the matter. I have the honour to wish you a very good-morning.' He bowed, and, turning away without observing the hand which the King had stretched out to him, he set off in my company for his chambers.

And that was how a great scandal threatened to affect the kingdom of Bohemia, and how the best plans of Mr Sherlock Holmes were beaten by a woman's wit. He used to make merry over the cleverness of women, but I have not heard him do it of late. And when he speaks of Irene Adler, or when he refers to her photograph, it is always under the honourable title of *the* woman.

# After reading

## Newsflash – Great detective fails!

**Imagine that news of Holmes's failure is reported in a brief newsflash: sum up the story in 50 words or less beginning, 'Great detective fails ...'**

**Compare your newsflash with those of others in the class. Talk about the differences and clear up any points of confusion.**

## Your personal response

**With a partner discuss the questions below.**

- What did you like about the story?
- What didn't you like?
- What question/s would you like to ask about the story?
- Were you surprised that Sherlock Holmes was out-witted by Irene Adler? Why/why not?

## It's a scandal!

**Think about the work you did on scandals before reading the story.**

- Which of the ingredients of a scandal can you find in this story?
- How do you think the story of 'A Scandal in Bohemia' would be different if it took place today?

## The structure of a crime story

At its most simple, the structure of many crime stories can be looked at in this way:

- at the beginning of the story there is order, all is well
- something happens, usually a crime, to disrupt that order
- the detective investigates and solves the case
- there is order again. Good has defeated evil.

Some people say that one of the reasons they enjoy reading crime stories like this is that order is always restored, good always triumphs over evil.

**Think about the structure of 'A Scandal in Bohemia' and discuss the questions below.**

- Irene Adler does not commit a crime – how does she 'disrupt' the order of things?
- Is order restored, in other words, are things put right, by the end of the story? You might want to consider the fact that Holmes fails, and the King of Bohemia's reaction to the outcome of the case.

## Why does Holmes fail?

It is very unusual for Holmes to fail to solve a case. In one story he mentions that he has failed only four times in over a thousand cases. So what goes wrong this time?

**Work in groups of four. Brainstorm all your ideas so far about why Holmes fails in this case.**

**Split into two pairs. One pair should look more closely at Holmes and the other at Irene Adler. Read the extracts below and on page 45 which relate to your character. What can you tell about this character? Do any of the extracts seem to suggest a reason for Holmes's failure?**

### Sherlock Holmes in the story

**Watson describing Holmes:**

It was not that he felt any emotion akin to love for Irene Adler. All emotions, and that one particularly, were abhorrent to his cold, precise but admirably balanced mind.

**Watson describing Holmes:**

Grit in a sensitive instrument, or a crack in one of his own high-power lenses, would not be more disturbing than a strong emotion in a nature such as his. And yet there was but one woman to him, and that woman was the late Irene Adler ...

**Holmes telling the story of Irene Adler's wedding:**

The bride gave me a sovereign and I mean to wear it on my watch chain in memory of the occasion.

**Watson ending the story:**

... how the best plans of Mr Sherlock Holmes were beaten by a woman's wit. He used to make merry over the cleverness of women, but I have not heard him do it of late.

## Irene Adler in the story

**Watson describing Irene Adler:**

Irene Adler, of dubious and questionable memory.

**The King of Bohemia describing Irene Adler:**

… the well-known adventuress …

… she has a soul of steel. She has the face of the most beautiful of women, and the mind of the most resolute of men. Rather than I should marry another woman, there are no lengths to which she would not go – none.

**Holmes describing Irene Adler:**

She is the daintiest thing under a bonnet on this planet.

Women are naturally secretive …

From what I have seen of the lady she seems indeed to be on a very different level to your majesty.

'THIS PHOTOGRAPH!'

## Beliefs about men and women

Now look at the chart below which lists some of the characteristics traditionally associated with men and women. For several centuries people had very fixed ideas about what men were like and what women were like.

Which of the beliefs seem to be supported by the extracts about your character? For example, does Holmes seem to be in control of his emotions? Are there any ways in which Irene Adler does not seem to conform to expectations about women at the time?

Feed back your findings to the other pair in your group of four. You should all make notes as they will be useful when you come to write your assignments.

| Beliefs about women | Beliefs about men |
| --- | --- |
| Passionate, prone to being jealous | Able to control their emotions |
| Passive (allow things to happen) | Active (make things happen) |
| Good at dealing with feelings | Good at being logical and scientific |
| Good at caring for others | Good at protecting and fighting for others |
| Secretive | Honest, loyal |
| Nice to look at, interested in making themselves pretty | Interested in being successful |
| Physically and mentally delicate, easy to upset, prone to getting ill | Physically and mentally strong, brave, good at making moral judgements |

## Why does Holmes fail? Reason versus passion

Kingsley Amis, in an essay titled 'Unreal Policemen' explained why he thought Conan Doyle had never put Sherlock Holmes into a relationship with a woman: 'The magnifying lens and the dozen red roses,' he wrote, 'belong to different worlds'.

**What do you think Amis means?**

**Think of a time when you felt strongly – angry, upset, jealous, in love. Do you think your emotions stopped you from thinking clearly? Did you make a mistake or misjudge a situation or a person because of strong feelings?**

**Does the story suggest that Holmes's feelings for Irene Adler affect his ability to be a good detective? Where is the evidence for this? You could start by looking at the quotations on pages 45 and 46.**

## The ending of the story – your personal response

**Listed below are some possible explanations for why Conan Doyle decided to end the story as he did. Think about how far each statement could be supported with evidence from the story.**

- Holmes has a low opinion of women and so underestimates Irene Adler.
- Conan Doyle makes Holmes a more realistic character by having him fail occasionally. In this case Holmes simply makes a mistake: being a master of disguises and knowing that Irene Adler has to act in her job as an opera singer, he should have realised that she was the 'slim youth' who wished him goodnight.
- Conan Doyle wanted the ending to be a surprise – he knew that most of his readers would expect Holmes to be successful, especially against a woman, because of their beliefs about men and women, and because of their knowledge of how detective stories usually work.
- Holmes is a little in love with Irene Adler. This emotion spoils his logical reasoning process and he can't think as clearly as usual.
- Irene Adler is simply cleverer than Holmes.
- Holmes isn't very interested in solving the case because he doesn't like the King of Bohemia.
- Although it seems as if Holmes has failed at the end, he hasn't really – order is restored and everyone is happy with the outcome.
- Irene Adler defeats Holmes because he has a very narrow view of women. He expects her to be emotional, not clever and logical.
- The point of the story is to show Holmes in an amusing light, rather than to intrigue the reader with the solving of a crime.

**Now decide on a statement that seems to you to sum up Conan Doyle's reasons for ending the story as he does. You could use one of the statements above, combine two or more statements, or make up your own.**

**Prepare a brief presentation for a small group, including evidence from the text, to explain why you think Conan Doyle chose to end the story the way he did. Each person in the group should give their presentation. You should then discuss your opinions and see if you can agree on a group statement.**

# The Red-Headed League

## Before reading

### Titles

Conan Doyle's titles are quite famous and have often been parodied (imitated in a humorous way) by other writers. Have a look at some of these titles of Holmes stories:

A Case of Identity
The Adventure of the Engineer's Thumb
The Second Stain
The Five Orange Pips
The Man with the Twisted Lip
A Study in Scarlet
The Adventure of the Copper Beeches
The Empty House
The Adventure of the Cardboard Box

Most of the Sherlock Holmes stories were originally published in a magazine (*The Strand Magazine*). Sherlock Holmes was one of the main things that made the magazine popular, so, each time there was a new story inside, Conan Doyle had to try to think of titles that would make someone want to buy the magazine.

**Do the titles you have just read succeed in making you want to read the story? Why/why not?**

**Make up your own title for a Sherlock Holmes story that would intrigue the reader and make them want to read on.**

The title of the story you are going to read is 'The Red-Headed League'. 'Red-Headed' means the same as 'red-haired'; 'league' means a group of people with a common interest, or a club.

**In a small group, discuss what the crime might be in this story – be as imaginative as you like!**

**Improvise a short scene in which the crime is committed. You could show your scene to the rest of the class.**

### During reading

**As you read the story you will find that at each** PAUSE **symbol there are questions or activities to help you to check your understanding of the story.**

## The Red-Headed League

I had called upon my friend, Mr Sherlock Holmes, one day in the autumn of last year, and found him in deep conversation with a very stout, florid-faced, elderly gentleman with fiery red hair. With an apology for my intrusion, I was about to withdraw, when Holmes pulled me abruptly into the room, and closed the door behind me.

'You could not possibly have come at a better time, my dear Watson,' he said cordially.

'I was afraid that you were engaged.'

'So I am. Very much so.'

'Then I can wait in the next room.'

'Not at all. This gentleman, Mr Wilson, has been my partner and helper in many of my most successful cases, and I have no doubt that he will be of the utmost use to me in yours also.'

The stout gentleman half rose from his chair, and gave a bob of greeting, with a quick little questioning glance from his small fat-encircled eyes.

'Try the settee,' said Holmes, relapsing into his armchair, and putting his fingertips together, as was his custom when in judicial moods. 'I know, my dear Watson, that you share my love of all that is bizarre and outside the conventions and humdrum routine of everyday life. You have shown your relish for it by the enthusiasm which has prompted you to chronicle, and, if you will excuse my saying so, somewhat to embellish so many of my own little adventures.'

'Your cases have indeed been of the greatest interest to me,' I observed.

'You will remember that I remarked the other day, just before we went into the very simple problem presented by Miss Mary Sutherland, that for strange effects and extraordinary combinations we must go to life itself, which is always far more daring than any effort of the imagination.'

'A proposition which I took the liberty of doubting.'

'You did, Doctor, but none the less you must come round to my view, for otherwise I shall keep on piling fact upon fact on you until your reason breaks down under them and acknowledges me to be right. Now, Mr Jabez Wilson here has been good enough to call upon me this morning, and to begin a narrative which promises to be one of the most singular which I have listened to for some time. You have heard me remark that the strangest and most unique things are very often connected not with the larger but with the smaller crimes, and occasionally, indeed, where there is room for doubt whether any positive crime has been committed. As far as I have heard it is impossible for me to say whether the present case is an instance of crime or not, but the course of events is certainly among the most singular that I have ever listened to. Perhaps, Mr Wilson, you would have the great kindness to recommence your narrative. I ask you not merely because my friend Dr Watson has not heard the opening part, but also because the peculiar nature of the story makes me anxious to have every possible detail from your lips. As a rule, when I have heard some slight indication of the course of events, I am able to guide myself by the thousands of other similar cases which occur to my memory. In the present instance I am forced to admit that the facts are, to the best of my belief, unique.'

**PAUSE**  Discuss your responses to the opening of the story. Use the questions below to get you started.

- How does Conan Doyle try to get the reader interested?
- What can you tell about the relationship between Holmes and Watson?
- How does Conan Doyle make the story seem realistic? (For example, why do you think he has Holmes refer to another of his cases – that of Miss Mary Sutherland, who appears in the story 'A Case of Identity'? Doyle often does this – sometimes the cases are from other stories, sometimes they are supposed to be cases that Watson hasn't written about.)

The portly client puffed out his chest with an appearance of some little pride and pulled a dirty and wrinkled newspaper from the inside pocket of his greatcoat. As he glanced down the advertisement column, with his head thrust forward and the paper flattened out upon his knee, I took a good look at the man and endeavoured, after the fashion of my companion, to read the indications which might be presented by his dress or appearance.

I did not gain very much, however, by my inspection. Our visitor bore every mark of being an average commonplace British tradesman, obese, pompous, and slow. He wore rather baggy grey shepherds' check trousers, a not over-clean black frock-coat, unbuttoned in the front, and a drab waistcoat with a heavy brassy Albert chain, and a square pierced bit of metal dangling down as an ornament. A frayed top-hat, and a faded brown overcoat with a wrinkled velvet collar lay upon a chair beside him. Altogether, look as I would, there was nothing remarkable about the man save his blazing red head, and the expression of extreme chagrin and discontent upon his features.

---

**PAUSE**    **What can you tell about this character from Watson's observations?**

---

Sherlock Holmes's quick eye took in my occupation, and he shook his head with a smile as he noticed my questioning glances. 'Beyond the obvious facts that he has at some time done manual labour, that he takes snuff, that he is a Freemason, that he has been in China, and that he has done a considerable amount of writing lately, I can deduce nothing else.'

Mr Jabez Wilson started up in his chair, with his forefinger upon the paper, but his eyes upon my companion.

'How, in the name of good fortune, did you know all that, Mr Holmes?' he asked. 'How did you know, for example, that I did manual labour? It's as true as gospel, and I began as a ship's carpenter.'

'Your hands, my dear sir. Your right hand is quite a size larger than your left. You have worked with it, and the muscles are more developed.'

'Well, the snuff, then, and the Freemasonry?'

'I won't insult your intelligence by telling you how I read that, especially as, rather against the strict rules of your order, you use an arc and compass breastpin.'

'Ah, of course, I forgot that. But the writing?'

'What else can be indicated by that right cuff so very shiny for five inches, and the left one with the smooth patch near the elbow where you rest it upon the desk?'

'Well, but China?'

'The fish that you have tattooed immediately above your right wrist could only have been done in China. I have made a small study of tattoo marks and have even contributed to the literature of the subject. That trick of staining the fishes' scales of a delicate pink is quite peculiar to China. When, in addition, I see a Chinese coin hanging from your watch-chain, the matter becomes even more simple.'

---

**PAUSE**    **Discuss what a reader might find enjoyable about this section. What does this section tell you about Holmes?**

---

Mr Jabez Wilson laughed heavily. 'Well, I never!' said he. 'I thought at first that you had done something clever, but I see that there was nothing in it, after all.'

'I begin to think, Watson,' said Holmes, 'that I make a mistake in explaining. '*Omne ignotum pro magnifico*'\*, you know, and my poor little reputation, such as it is, will suffer shipwreck if I am so candid. Can you not find the advertisement, Mr Wilson?'

'Yes, I have got it now,' he answered, with his thick, red finger planted halfway down the column. 'Here it is. This is what began it all. You just read it for yourself, sir.'

I took the paper from him and read as follows.

> **TO THE RED-HEADED LEAGUE** – On account of the bequest of the late Ezekiah Hopkins, of Lebanon, Pennsylvania, U. S. A., there is now another vacancy open which entitles a member of the League to a salary of four pounds a week for purely nominal services. All red-headed men who are sound in body and mind, and above the age of twenty-one years, are eligible. Apply in person on Monday, at eleven o'clock, to Duncan Ross, at the  offices of the League, 7 Pope's Court, Fleet Street.

'What on earth does this mean?' I ejaculated, after I had twice read over the extraordinary announcement.

Holmes chuckled, and wriggled in his chair, as was his habit when in high spirits. 'It is a little off the beaten track, isn't it?' said he. 'And now, Mr Wilson, off you go at scratch, and tell us all about yourself, your household, and the effect which this advertisement had upon your fortunes. You will first make a note, Doctor, of the paper and the date.'

'It is *The Morning Chronicle* of April 27, 1890. Just two months ago.'

'Very good. Now, Mr Wilson?'

\* *everything that is unknown is taken for magnificent*

---

'Well, it is just as I have been telling you, Mr Sherlock Holmes,' said Jabez Wilson, mopping his forehead; 'I have a small pawnbroker's business at Coburg Square, near the City. It's not a very large affair, and of late years it has not done more than just give me a living. I used to be able to keep two assistants, but now I only keep one; and I would have a job to pay him, but that he is willing to come for half wages so as to learn the business.'

'What is the name of this obliging youth?' asked Sherlock Holmes.

'His name is Vincent Spaulding, and he's not such a youth, either. It's hard to say his age. I should not wish a smarter assistant, Mr Holmes; and I know very well that he could better himself and earn twice what I am able to give him. But, after all, if he is satisfied, why should I put ideas in his head?'

'Why, indeed? You seem most fortunate in having an employee who comes under the full market price. It is not a common experience among employers in this age. I don't know that your assistant is not as remarkable as your advertisement.'

'Oh, he has his faults, too,' said Mr Wilson. 'Never was such a fellow for photography. Snapping away with a camera when he ought to be improving his mind, and then diving down into the cellar like a rabbit into its hole to develop his pictures. That is his main fault, but on the whole he's a good worker. There's no vice in him.'

**PAUSE**    **Discuss your impressions of Vincent Spaulding.**

'He is still with you, I presume?'

'Yes, sir. He and a girl of fourteen, who does a bit of simple cooking, and keeps the place clean – that's all I have in the house, for I am a widower and never had any family. We live very quietly, sir, the three of us; and we keep a roof over our heads and pay our debts, if we do nothing more.

'The first thing that put us out was that advertisement. Spaulding, he came down into the office just this day eight weeks with this very paper in his hand, and he says:

'"I wish to the Lord, Mr Wilson, that I was a red-headed man."

'"Why that?" I asks.

'"Why," says he, "here's another vacancy on the League of the Red-Headed Men. It's worth quite a little fortune to any man who gets it, and I understand that there are more vacancies than there are men, so that the trustees are at their wit's end what to do with the money. If my hair would only change colour, here's a nice little crib all ready for me to step into."

'"Why, what is it, then?" I asked. You see. Mr Holmes, I am a very stay-at-home man, and as my business came to me instead of my having to go to it, I was often weeks on end without putting my foot over the door-mat. In that way I didn't know much of what was going on outside, and I was always glad of a bit of news.

'"Have you never heard of the League of the Red-Headed Men?" he asked with his eyes open.

'"Never."

'"Why, I wonder at that, for you are eligible yourself for one of the vacancies."

'"And what are they worth?" I asked.

'"Oh, merely a couple of hundred a year, but the work is slight, and it need not interfere very much with one's other occupations."

'Well, you can easily think that that made me prick up my ears, for the business has not been over good for some years, and an extra couple of hundred would have been very handy.

'"Tell me all about it," said I.

'"Well," said he, showing me the advertisement, "you can see for yourself that the League has a vacancy, and there is the address where you should apply for particulars. As far as I can make out, the League was founded by an American millionaire, Ezekiah Hopkins, who was very peculiar in his ways. He was himself red-headed, and he had a great sympathy for all red-headed men; so, when he died it was found that he had left his enormous fortune in the hands of trustees, with instructions to apply the interest to the providing of easy berths to men whose hair is of that colour. From all I hear it is splendid pay, and very little to do."

'"But," said I, "there would be millions of red-headed men who would apply."

'"Not so many as you might think," he answered. "You see it is really confined to Londoners, and to grown men. This American had started from London when he was young, and he wanted to do the old town a good turn. Then, again, I have heard it is no use your applying if your hair is light red, or dark red, or anything but real bright, blazing, fiery red. Now, if you cared to apply, Mr Wilson, you would just walk in; but perhaps it would hardly be worth your while to put yourself out of the way for the sake of a few hundred pounds."

'Now, it is a fact, gentlemen, as you may see for yourselves, that my hair is of a very full and rich tint, so that it seemed to me that, if there was to be any competition in the matter, I stood as good a chance as any man that I had ever met. Vincent Spaulding seemed to know so much about it that I thought he might prove useful, so I just ordered him to put up the shutters for the day and to come right away with me. He was very willing to have a holiday, so we shut the business up, and started off for the address that was given us in the advertisement.

'I never hope to see such a sight as that again, Mr Holmes. From north, south, east, and west every man who had a shade of red in his hair had tramped into the city to answer the advertisement. Fleet Street was choked with red-headed folk, and Pope's Court looked like a coster's* orange barrow. I should not have thought there were so many in the whole country as were brought together by that single advertisement. Every shade of colour they were – straw, lemon, orange, brick, Irish-setter, liver, clay; but, as Spaulding said, there were not many who had the real vivid flame-coloured tint. When I saw how many were waiting, I would have given it up in despair; but Spaulding would not hear of it. How he did it I could not imagine, but he pushed and pulled and butted until he got me through the crowd, and right up to the steps which led to the office. There was a double stream upon the stair, some going up in hope, and some coming back dejected; but we wedged in as well as we could, and soon found ourselves in the office.'

'Your experience has been a most entertaining one,' remarked Holmes as his client paused and refreshed his memory with a huge pinch of snuff. 'Pray continue your very interesting statement.'

'There was nothing in the office but a couple of wooden chairs and a deal table, behind which sat a small man, with a head that was even redder than mine. He said a few words to each candidate as he came up, and then he always managed to find some fault in them which would disqualify them. Getting a vacancy did not seem to be such a very easy matter, after all. However, when our turn came, the little man was much more favourable to me than to any of the others, and he closed the door as we entered, so that he might have a private word with us.

'"This is Mr Jabez Wilson," said my assistant, "and he is willing to fill a vacancy in the League."

'"And he is admirably suited for it," the other answered. "He has every requirement. I cannot recall when I have seen anything so fine." He took a step backward, cocked his head on one side, and gazed at my hair until I felt quite bashful. Then suddenly he plunged forward, wrung my hand, and congratulated me warmly on my success.

'"It would be injustice to hesitate," said he. "You will, however, I am sure, excuse me for taking an obvious precaution." With that he seized my hair in both his hands, and tugged until I yelled with the pain. "There is water in your eyes," said he as he released me. "I perceive that all is as it should be. But we have to be careful, for we have twice been deceived by wigs and once by paint. I could tell you tales of cobbler's wax which would disgust you with human nature." He stepped over to the window and shouted through it at the top of his voice that the vacancy was filled. A groan of disappointment came up from below, and the folk all trooped away in different directions until there was not a red-head to be seen except my own and that of the manager.

'"My name," said he, "is Mr Duncan Ross, and I am myself one of the pensioners upon the fund left by our noble benefactor. Are you a married man, Mr Wilson? Have you a family?"

'I answered that I had not.

'His face fell immediately.

'"Dear me!" he said gravely, "that is very serious indeed! I am sorry to hear you say that. The fund was, of course, for the propagation and spread of the red-heads as well as for their maintenance. It is exceedingly unfortunate that you should be a bachelor."

'My face lengthened at this, Mr Holmes, for I thought that I was not to have the vacancy after all; but after thinking it over for a few minutes he said that it would be all right.

'"In the case of another" said he, "the objection might be fatal, but we must stretch a point in favour of a man with such a head of hair as yours. When shall you be able to enter upon your new duties?"

'"Well, it is a little awkward, for I have a business already," said I.

'"Oh, never mind about that, Mr Wilson!" said Vincent Spaulding. "I should be able to look after that for you."

'"What would be the hours?" I asked.

'"Ten to two."

'Now a pawnbroker's business is mostly done of an evening, Mr Holmes, especially Thursday and Friday evening, which is just before pay-day; so it would suit me very well to earn a little in the mornings. Besides, I knew that my assistant was a good man, and that he would see to anything that turned up.

'"That would suit me very well," said I. "And the pay?"

'"Is four pounds a week."

---

* A coster (costermonger) sold fruit and vegetables in the street, from a barrow

'"And the work?"

'"Is purely nominal."

'"What do you call purely nominal?"

'"Well, you have to be in the office, or at least in the building, the whole time. If you leave, you forfeit your whole position forever. The will is very clear upon that point. You don't comply with the conditions if you budge from the office during that time."

'"It's only four hours a day, and I should not think of leaving," said I.

'"No excuse will avail,' said Mr Duncan Ross; 'neither sickness, nor business, nor anything else. There you must stay, or you lose your billet."

'"And the work?"

'"Is to copy out the *Encyclopedia Britannica*. There is the first volume of it in that press. You must find your own ink, pens, and blotting-paper, but we provide this table and chair. Will you be ready tomorrow?"

'"Certainly," I answered.

'"Then, good-bye, Mr Jabez Wilson, and let me congratulate you once more on the important position which you have been fortunate enough to gain." He bowed me out of the room and I went home with my assistant, hardly knowing what to say or do, I was so pleased at my own good fortune.

---

**PAUSE**    **With a partner, discuss your predictions for the rest of Mr Jabez Wilson's story.**

---

'Well, I thought over the matter all day, and by evening I was in low spirits again; for I had quite persuaded myself that the whole affair must be some great hoax or fraud, though what its object might be I could not imagine. It seemed altogether past belief that anyone could make such a will, or that they would pay such a sum for doing anything so simple as copying out the *Encyclopedia Britannica*. Vincent Spaulding did what he could to cheer me up, but by bedtime I had reasoned myself out of the whole thing. However, in the morning I determined to have a look at it anyhow, so I bought a penny bottle of ink, and with a quill-pen, and seven sheets of foolscap paper, I started off for Pope's Court.

'Well, to my surprise and delight, everything was as right as possible. The table was set out ready for me, and Mr Duncan Ross was there to see that I got fairly to work. He started me off upon the letter A, and then he left me; but he would drop in from time to time to see that all was right with me. At two o'clock he bade me good day, complimented me upon the amount that I had written, and locked the door of the office after me.

'This went on day after day, Mr Holmes, and on Saturday the manager came in and planked down four golden sovereigns for my week's work. It was the same next week, and the same the week after. Every morning I was there at ten, and every afternoon I left at two. By degrees Mr Duncan Ross took to coming in only once of a morning, and then, after a time, he did not come in at all. Still, of course, I never dared to leave the room for an instant, for I was not sure when he might come, and the billet was such a good one, and suited me so well, that I would not risk the loss of it.

'Eight weeks passed away like this, and I had written about Abbots and Archery and Armour and Architecture and Attica, and hoped with diligence that I might get on to the B's before very long. It cost me something in foolscap, and I had pretty nearly filled a shelf with my writings. And then suddenly the whole business came to an end.'

'To an end?'

'Yes, sir. And no later than this morning. I went to my work as usual at ten o'clock, but the door was shut and locked, with a little square of cardboard hammered on to the middle of the panel with a tack. Here it is, and you can read for yourself.'

He held up a piece of white cardboard, about the size of a sheet of note-paper. It read in this fashion:

---

**THE RED-HEADED LEAGUE IS DISSOLVED.**

**Oct. 9, 1890.**

---

Sherlock Holmes and I surveyed this curt announcement and the rueful face behind it, until the comical side of the affair so completely over-topped every other consideration that we both burst out into a roar of laughter.

'I cannot see that there is anything very funny,' cried our client, flushing up to the roots of his flaming head. 'If you can do nothing better than laugh at me, I can go elsewhere.'

---

'No, no,' cried Holmes, shoving him back into the chair from which he had half risen. 'I really wouldn't miss your case for the world. It is most refreshingly unusual. But there is, if you will excuse my saying so, something just a little funny about it. Pray what steps did you take when you found the card upon the door?'

**PAUSE**     **Discuss what you think of the way Holmes and Watson treat Mr Jabez Wilson.**

'I was staggered, sir. I did not know what to do. Then I called at the offices round, but none of them seemed to know anything about it. Finally, I went to the landlord, who is an accountant living on the ground floor, and I asked him if he could tell me what had become of the Red-Headed League. He said that he had never heard of any such body. Then I asked him who Mr Duncan Ross was. He answered that the name was new to him.

'"Well," said I, "the gentleman at No. 4."

'"What, the red-headed man?"

'"Yes."

'"Oh," said he, "his name was William Morris. He was a solicitor and was using my room as a temporary convenience until his new premises were ready. He moved out yesterday."

'"Where could I find him?"

'"Oh, at his new offices. He did tell me the address. Yes, 17 King Edward Street, near St. Paul's."

THE DOOR WAS SHUT AND LOCKED

'I started off, Mr Holmes, but when I got to that address it was a manufactory of artificial knee-caps, and no one in it had ever heard of either Mr William Morris or Mr Duncan Ross.'

'And what did you do then?' asked Holmes.

'I went home to Saxe-Coburg Square, and I took the advice of my assistant. But he could not help me in any way. He could only say that if I waited I should hear by post. But that was not quite good enough, Mr Holmes. I did not wish to lose such a place without a struggle, so, as I had heard that you were good enough to give advice to poor folk who were in need of it, I came right away to you.'

'And you did very wisely,' said Holmes. 'Your case is an exceedingly remarkable one, and I shall be happy to look into it. From what you have told me I think that it is possible that graver issues hang from it than might at first sight appear.'

'Grave enough!' said Mr Jabez Wilson. 'Why, I have lost four pound a week.'

'As far as you are personally concerned,' remarked Holmes, 'I do not see that you have any grievance against this extraordinary league. On the contrary, you are, as I understand, richer by some thirty pounds, to say nothing of the minute knowledge which you have gained on every subject which comes under the letter A. You have lost nothing by them.'

'No, sir. But I want to find out about them, and who they are, and what their object was in playing this prank – if it was a prank – upon me. It was a pretty expensive joke for them, for it cost them two and thirty pounds.'

'We shall endeavour to clear up these points for you. And, first, one or two questions, Mr Wilson. This assistant of yours who first called your attention to the advertisement – how long had he been with you?'

'About a month then.'

'How did he come?'

'In answer to an advertisement.'

'Was he the only applicant?'

'No, I had a dozen.'

'Why did you pick him?'

'Because he was handy, and would come cheap.'

'At half-wages, in fact.'

'Yes.'

'What is he like, this Vincent Spaulding?'

'Small, stout-built, very quick in his ways, no hair on his face, though he's not short of thirty. Has a white splash of acid upon his forehead.'

Holmes sat up in his chair in considerable excitement. 'I thought as much,' said he. 'Have you ever observed that his ears are pierced for earrings?'

'Yes, sir. He told me that a gypsy had done it for him when he was a lad.'

'Hum!' said Holmes, sinking back in deep thought. 'He is still with you?'

'Oh, yes, sir; I have only just left him.'

'And has your business been attended to in your absence?'

'Nothing to complain of, sir. There's never very much to do of a morning.'

'That will do, Mr Wilson. I shall be happy to give you an opinion upon the subject in the course of a day or two. Today is Saturday, and I hope that by Monday we may come to a conclusion.'

HE CURLED HIMSELF UP
IN HIS CHAIR

'Well, Watson,' said Holmes when our visitor had left us, 'what do you make of it all?'

'I make nothing of it,' I answered, frankly. 'It is a most mysterious business.'

'As a rule,' said Holmes, 'the more bizarre a thing is the less mysterious it proves to be. It is your commonplace, featureless crimes which are really puzzling, just as a commonplace face is the most difficult to identify. But I must be prompt over this matter.'

'What are you going to do, then?' I asked.

'To smoke,' he answered. 'It is quite a three-pipe problem, and I beg that you won't speak to me for fifty minutes.' He curled himself up in his chair, with his thin knees drawn up to his hawk-like nose, and there he sat with his eyes closed and his black clay pipe thrusting out like the bill of some strange bird. I had come to the conclusion that he had dropped asleep, and indeed was nodding myself, when he suddenly sprang out of his chair with the gesture of a man who has made up his mind, and put his pipe down upon the mantelpiece.

'Sarasate plays at the St. James's Hall this afternoon,' he remarked. 'What do you think, Watson? Could your patients spare you for a few hours?'

'I have nothing to do today. My practice is never very absorbing.'

'Then put on your hat and come. I am going through the City first, and we can have some lunch on the way. I observe that there is a good deal of German music on the programme which is rather more to my taste than Italian or French. It is introspective, and I want to introspect. Come along!'

We travelled by the Underground as far as Aldersgate; and a short walk took us to Saxe-Coburg Square, the scene of the singular story which we had listened to in the morning. It was a pokey, little, shabby-genteel place, where four lines of dingy two-storied brick houses looked out into a small railed-in enclosure, where a lawn of weedy grass and a few clumps of faded laurel bushes made a hard fight against a smoke-laden and uncongenial atmosphere. Three gilt balls and a brown board with JABEZ WILSON in white letters upon a corner house, announced the place where our red-headed client carried on his business. Sherlock Holmes stopped in front of it with his head on one side and looked it all over, with his eyes shining brightly between puckered lids. Then he walked slowly up the street, and then down again to the corner, still looking keenly at the houses. Finally he returned to the pawnbroker's, and, having thumped vigorously upon the pavement with his stick two or three times, he went up to the door and knocked. It was instantly opened by a bright-looking, clean-shaven young fellow, who asked him to step in.

'Thank you,' said Holmes, 'I only wished to ask you how you would go from here to the Strand.'

'Third right, fourth left,' answered the assistant promptly, closing the door.

'Smart fellow, that,' observed Holmes as we walked away. 'He is, in my judgment, the fourth smartest man in London, and for daring I am not sure that he has not a claim to be third. I have known something of him before.'

'Evidently,' said I, 'Mr Wilson's assistant counts for a good deal in this mystery of The Red-Headed League. I am sure that you inquired your way merely in order that you might see him.'

'Not him.'

'What then?'

'The knees of his trousers.'

'And what did you see?'

'What I expected to see.'

'Why did you beat the pavement?'

'My dear Doctor, this is a time for observation, not for talk. We are spies in an enemy's country. We know something of Saxe-Coburg Square. Let us now explore the parts which lie behind it.'

| | |
|---|---|
| **PAUSE** | **Talk about how this dialogue between Holmes and Watson helps to make the reader curious about the solution to the mystery.** |
| | **What do you think Holmes might have discovered that will help him to solve the mystery?** |

The road in which we found ourselves as we turned round the corner from the retired Saxe-Coburg Square presented as great a contrast to it as the front of a picture does to the back. It was one of the main arteries which conveyed the traffic of the City to the north and west. The roadway was blocked with the immense stream of commerce flowing in a double tide inwards and outwards, while the footpaths were black with the hurrying swarm of pedestrians. It was difficult to realize as we looked at the line of fine shops and stately business premises that they really abutted on the other side upon the faded and stagnant square which we had just quitted.

'Let me see,' said Holmes, standing at the corner and glancing along the line, 'I should like just to remember the order of the houses here. It is a hobby of mine to have an exact knowledge of London. There is Mortimer's, the tobacconist, the little newspaper shop, the Coburg branch of the City and Suburban Bank, the Vegetarian Restaurant, and McFarlane's carriage-building depot. That carries us right on to the other block. And now, Doctor, we've done our work, so it's time we had some play. A sandwich and a cup of coffee, and then off to violin land, where all is sweetness and delicacy and harmony, and there are no red-headed clients to vex us with their conundrums.'

My friend was an enthusiastic musician, being himself not only a very capable performer, but a composer of no ordinary merit. All the afternoon he sat in the stalls wrapped in the most perfect happiness, gently waving his long, thin fingers in time to the music, while his gently smiling face and his languid, dreamy eyes were as unlike those of Holmes, the sleuth-hound, Holmes the relentless, keen-witted, ready-handed criminal agent, as it was possible to conceive. In his singular character the dual nature alternately asserted itself, and his extreme exactness and astuteness represented, as I have often thought, the reaction against the poetic and contemplative mood which occasionally predominated in him. The swing of his nature took him from extreme languor to devouring energy; and, as I knew well, he was never so truly formidable as when, for days on end, he had been lounging in his armchair amid his improvisations and his black-letter editions. Then it was that the lust of the chase would suddenly come upon him, and that his brilliant reasoning power would rise to the level of intuition, until those who were unacquainted with his methods would look askance at him as on a man whose knowledge was not that of other mortals. When I saw him that afternoon so enwrapped in the music at St. James's Hall I felt that an evil time might be coming upon those whom he had set himself to hunt down.

'You want to go home, no doubt, Doctor,' he remarked as we emerged.

'Yes, it would be as well.'

'And I have some business to do which will take some hours. This business at Coburg Square is serious.'

'Why serious?'

'A considerable crime is in contemplation. I have every reason to believe that we shall be in time to stop it. But today being Saturday rather complicates matters. I shall want your help tonight.'

'At what time?'

'Ten will be early enough.'

'I shall be at Baker Street at ten.'

'Very well. And, I say, Doctor! there may be some little danger, so kindly put your army revolver in your pocket.' He waved his hand, turned on his heel, and disappeared in an instant among the crowd.

I trust that I am not more dense than my neighbours, but I was always oppressed with a sense of my own stupidity in my dealings with Sherlock Holmes. Here I had heard what he had heard, I had seen what he had seen, and yet from his words it was evident that he saw clearly not only what had happened, but what was about to happen, while to me the whole business was still confused and grotesque. As I drove home to my house in Kensington I thought over it all, from the extraordinary story of the red-headed copier of the *Encyclopedia* down to the visit to Saxe-Coburg Square, and the ominous words with which he had parted from me. What was this nocturnal expedition, and why should I go armed? Where were we going, and what were we to do? I had the hint from Holmes that this smooth-faced pawnbroker's assistant was a formidable man – a man who might play a deep game. I tried to puzzle it out, but gave it up in despair and set the matter aside until night should bring an explanation.

**PAUSE**    **Can you do better than Watson? With a partner, try to solve the mystery with the information you have so far. Hint: a clue is hidden in the list of shops Holmes mentions in this section.**

It was a quarter-past nine when I started from home and made my way across the Park, and so through Oxford Street to Baker Street. Two hansoms were standing at the door, and, as I entered the passage I heard the sound of voices from above. On entering his room I found Holmes in animated conversation with two men, one of whom I recognized as Peter Jones, the official police agent, while the other was a long, thin, sad-faced man, with a very shiny hat and oppressively respectable frock-coat.

'Ha! our party is complete,' said Holmes, buttoning up his pea-jacket and taking his heavy hunting-crop from the rack. 'Watson, I think you know Mr Jones, of Scotland Yard? Let me introduce you to Mr Merryweather, who is to be our companion in tonight's adventure.'

'We're hunting in couples again, Doctor, you see,' said Jones in his consequential way. 'Our friend here is a wonderful man for starting a chase. All he wants is an old dog to help him to do the running down.'

'I hope a wild goose may not prove to be the end of our chase,' observed Mr Merryweather gloomily.

'You may place considerable confidence in Mr Holmes, sir,' said the police agent loftily. 'He has his own little methods, which are, if he won't mind my saying so, just a little too theoretical and fantastic, but he has the makings of a detective in him. It is not too much to say that once or twice, as in that business of the Sholto murder and the Agra treasure, he has been more nearly correct than the official force.'

'Oh, if you say so, Mr Jones, it is all right,' said the stranger with deference. 'Still, I confess that I miss my rubber.* It is the first Saturday night for seven-and-twenty years that I have not had my rubber.'

'I think you will find,' said Sherlock Holmes, 'that you will play for a higher stake tonight than you have ever done yet, and that the play will be more exciting. For you, Mr Merryweather, the stake will be some thirty thousand pounds; and for you, Jones, it will be the man upon whom you wish to lay your hands.'

'John Clay, the murderer, thief, smasher, and forger. He's a young man, Mr Merryweather, but he is at the head of his profession, and I would rather have my bracelets on him than on any criminal in London. He's a remarkable man, is young John Clay. His grandfather was a royal duke, and he himself has been to Eton and Oxford. His brain is as cunning as his fingers, and though we meet signs of him at every turn, we never know where to find the man himself. He'll crack a crib in Scotland one week, and be raising money to build an orphanage in Cornwall the next. I've been on his track for years and have never set eyes on him yet.'

'I hope that I may have the pleasure of introducing you tonight. I've had one or two little turns also with Mr John Clay, and I agree with you that he is at the head of his profession. It is past ten, however, and quite time that we started. If you two will take the first hansom, Watson and I will follow in the second.'

Sherlock Holmes was not very communicative during the long drive and lay back in the cab humming the tunes which he had heard in the afternoon. We rattled through an endless labyrinth of gas-lit streets until we emerged into Farringdon Street.

'We are close there now,' my friend remarked. 'This fellow Merryweather is a bank director, and personally interested in the matter. I thought it as well to have Jones with us also. He is not a bad fellow, though an absolute imbecile in his profession. He has one positive virtue. He is as brave as a bulldog and as tenacious as a lobster if he gets his claws upon anyone. Here we are, and they are waiting for us.'

We had reached the same crowded thoroughfare in which we had found ourselves in the morning. Our cabs were dismissed, and, following the guidance of Mr Merryweather, we passed down a narrow passage, and through a side door, which he opened for us. Within there was a small corridor, which ended in a very massive iron gate. This also was opened, and led down a flight of winding stone steps, which terminated at another formidable gate. Mr Merryweather stopped to light a lantern, and then conducted us down a dark, earth-smelling passage, and so, after opening a third door, into a huge vault or cellar, which was piled all round with crates and massive boxes.

'You are not very vulnerable from above,' Holmes remarked as he held up the lantern and gazed about him.

'Nor from below,' said Mr Merryweather, striking his stick upon the flags which lined the floor. 'Why, dear me, it sounds quite hollow!' he remarked, looking up in surprise.

'I must really ask you to be a little more quiet!' said Holmes severely. 'You have already imperilled the whole success of our expedition. Might I beg that you would have the goodness to sit down upon one of those boxes, and not to interfere?'

The solemn Mr Merryweather perched himself upon a crate, with a very injured expression upon his face, while Holmes fell upon his knees upon the floor and, with the lantern and a magnifying lens, began to examine minutely the cracks between the stones. A few seconds sufficed to satisfy him, for he sprang to his feet again and put his glass in his pocket.

'We have at least an hour before us,' he remarked, 'for they can hardly take any steps until the good pawnbroker is safely in bed. Then, they will not lose a minute, for the sooner they do their work the longer time they will have for their escape. We are at present, Doctor – as no doubt you have divined – in the cellar of the City branch of one of the principal London banks. Mr Merryweather is the chairman of directors, and he will explain to you that there are reasons why the more daring criminals of London should take a considerable interest in this cellar at present.'

'It is our French gold,' whispered the director. 'We have had several warnings that an attempt might be made upon it.'

'Your French gold?'

'Yes. We had occasion some months ago to strengthen our resources and borrowed for that purpose thirty thousand napoleons from the Bank of France. It has become known that we have never had occasion to unpack the money, and that it is still lying in our cellar. The crate upon which I sit contains two thousand napoleons packed between layers of lead foil. Our reserve of bullion is much larger at present than is usually kept in a single branch office, and the directors have had misgivings upon the subject.'

'Which were very well justified,' observed Holmes. 'And now it is time that we arranged our little plans. I expect that within an hour matters will come to a head. In the meantime Mr Merryweather, we must put the screen over that dark lantern.'

'And sit in the dark?'

'I am afraid so. I had brought a pack of cards in my pocket, and I thought that, as we were a *partie carrée,*\* you might have your rubber after all. But I see that the enemy's preparations have gone so far that we cannot risk the presence of a light. And, first of all, we must choose our positions. These are daring men, and though we shall take them at a disadvantage, they may do us some harm, unless we are careful. I shall stand behind this crate, and do you conceal yourself behind those. Then, when I flash a light upon them, close in swiftly. If they fire, Watson, have no compunction about shooting them down.'

I placed my revolver, cocked, upon the top of the wooden case behind which I crouched. Holmes shot the slide across the front of his lantern and left us in pitch darkness – such an absolute darkness as I have never before experienced. The smell of hot metal remained to assure us that the light was still there, ready to flash out at a moment's notice. To me, with my nerves worked up to a pitch of expectancy, there was something depressing and subduing in the sudden gloom, and in the cold, dank air of the vault.

'They have but one retreat,' whispered Holmes. 'That is back through the house into Saxe-Coburg Square. I hope that you have done what I asked you, Jones?'

'I have an Inspector and two officers waiting at the front door.'

'Then we have stopped all the holes. And now we must be silent and wait.'

What a time it seemed! From comparing notes afterwards it was but an hour and a quarter, yet it appeared to me that the night must have almost gone, and the dawn be breaking above us. My limbs were weary and stiff, for I feared to change my position; yet my nerves were worked up to the highest pitch of tension, and my hearing was so acute that I could not only hear the gentle breathing of my companions, but I could distinguish the deeper, heavier in-breath of the bulky Jones from the thin, sighing note of the bank director. From my position I could look over the case in the direction of the floor. Suddenly my eyes caught the glint of a light.

At first it was but a lurid spark upon the stone pavement. Then it lengthened out until it became a yellow line, and then, without any warning or sound, a gash seemed to open and a hand appeared; a white, almost womanly hand, which felt about in the centre of the little area of light. For a minute or more the hand, with its writhing fingers, protruded out of the floor. Then it was withdrawn as suddenly as it appeared, and all was dark again save the single lurid spark which marked a chink between the stones.

Its disappearance, however, was but momentary. With a rending, tearing sound, one of the broad, white stones turned over upon its side and left a square, gaping hole, through which streamed the light of a lantern. Over the edge there peeped a clean-cut, boyish face, which looked keenly about it, and then, with a hand on either side of the aperture, drew itself shoulder high and waist-high until one knee rested upon the edge. In another instant he stood at the side of the hole and was hauling after him a companion, lithe and small like himself, with a pale face and a shock of very red hair.

'It's all clear,' he whispered. 'Have you the chisel and the bags? Great Scott! Jump, Archie, jump, and I'll swing for it!'

Sherlock Holmes had sprung out and seized the intruder by the collar. The other dived down the hole, and I heard the sound of rending cloth as Jones clutched at his skirts. The light flashed upon the barrel of a revolver, but Holmes's hunting crop came down on the man's wrist, and the pistol clinked upon the stone floor.

'It's no use, John Clay,' said Holmes blandly. 'You have no chance at all.'

'So I see,' the other answered with the utmost coolness. 'I fancy that my pal is all right, though I see you have got his coat-tails.'

'There are three men waiting for him at the door,' said Holmes.

'Oh, indeed. You seem to have done the thing very completely. I must compliment you.'

'And I you,' Holmes answered. 'Your red-headed idea was very new and effective.'

* 'rubber' means a game of Bridge – which is a kind of card game
partie carree = party of four

'IT'S NO USE, JOHN CLAY'

**PAUSE**   **Talk about what you think of the way Holmes treats John Clay in this section.**

**Remember the way Holmes treated Mr Jabez Wilson when he told his story – who does Holmes seem to have more respect for? Why do you think this is?**

'You'll see your pal again presently,' said Jones. 'He's quicker at climbing down holes than I am. Just hold out while I fix the derbies.'*

'I beg that you will not touch me with your filthy hands,' remarked our prisoner as the handcuffs clattered upon his wrists. 'You may not be aware that I have royal blood in my veins. Have the goodness, also, when you address me always to say 'sir' and 'please'.'

'All right,' said Jones, with a stare and a snigger. 'Well, would you please, sir, march upstairs, where we can get a cab to carry your highness to the police-station?'

'That is better,' said John Clay serenely. He made a sweeping bow to the three of us and walked quietly off in the custody of the detective.

'Really, Mr Holmes,' said Mr Merryweather as we followed them from the cellar, 'I do not know how the bank can thank you or repay you. There is no doubt that you have detected and defeated in the most complete manner one of the most determined attempts at bank robbery that have ever come within my experience.'

'I have had one or two little scores of my own to settle with Mr John Clay,' said Holmes. 'I have been at some small expense over this matter, which I shall expect the bank to refund, but beyond that I am amply repaid by having had an experience which is in many ways unique, and by hearing the very remarkable narrative of the Red-Headed League.'

'You see, Watson,' he explained in the early hours of the morning, as we sat over a glass of whisky and soda in Baker Street, 'it was perfectly obvious from the first that the only possible object of this rather fantastic business of the advertisement of the League, and the copying of the *Encyclopedia*, must be to get this not over-bright pawnbroker out of the way for a number of hours every day. It was a curious way of managing it, but really, it would be difficult to suggest a better. The method was no doubt suggested to Clay's ingenious mind by the colour of his accomplice's hair. The four pounds a week was a lure which must draw him, and what was it to them, who were playing for thousands? They put in the advertisement, one rogue has the temporary office, the other rogue incites the man to apply for it, and together they manage to secure his absence every morning in the week. From the time that I heard of the assistant having come for half-wages, it was obvious to me that he had some strong motive for securing the situation.'

'But how could you guess what the motive was?'

'Had there been women in the house, I should have suspected a mere vulgar intrigue. That, however, was out of the question. The man's business was a small one, and there was nothing in his house which could account for such elaborate preparations, and such an expenditure as they were at. It must then be something out of the house. What could it be? I thought of the assistant's fondness for photography, and his trick of vanishing into the cellar. The cellar! There was the end of this tangled clue. Then I made inquiries as to this mysterious assistant, and found that I had to deal with one of the coolest and most daring criminals in London. He was doing something in the cellar – something which took many hours a day for months on end. What could it be, once more? I could think of nothing save that he was running a tunnel to some other building.

'So far I had got when we went to visit the scene of action. I surprised you by beating upon the pavement with my stick. I was ascertaining whether the cellar stretched out in front or behind. It was not in front. Then I rang the bell, and, as I hoped, the assistant answered it. We have had some skirmishes, but we had never set eyes upon each other before. I hardly looked at his face. His knees were what I wished to see. You must yourself have remarked how worn, wrinkled, and stained they were. They spoke of those hours of burrowing. The only remaining point was what they were burrowing for. I walked round the corner, saw the City and Suburban Bank abutted on our friend's premises, and felt that I had solved my problem. When you drove home after the concert I called upon Scotland Yard and upon the chairman of the bank directors, with the result that you have seen.'

'And how could you tell that they would make their attempt tonight?' I asked.

'Well, when they closed their League offices that was a sign that they cared no longer about Mr Jabez Wilson's presence – in other words, that they had completed their tunnel. But it was essential that they should use it soon, as it might be discovered, or the bullion might be removed. Saturday would suit them better than any other day, as it would give them two days for their escape. For all these reasons I expected them to come tonight.'

'You reasoned it out beautifully,' I exclaimed in unfeigned admiration. 'It is so long a chain, and yet every link rings true.'

'It saved me from ennui,'* he answered, yawning. 'Alas! I already feel it closing in upon me. My life is spent in one long effort to escape from the commonplaces of existence. These little problems help me to do so.'

'And you are a benefactor of the race,' said I.

He shrugged his shoulders. 'Well, perhaps, after all, it is of some little use,' he remarked. '"*L'homme c'est rien – l'oeuvre c'est tout,*"* as Gustave Flaubert wrote to George Sand.'

> * Derbies = handcuffs
> ennui = boredom;
> 'L'homme c'est rien - l' oeuvre c'est tout,' should be 'l'homme n'est rien – l'oeuvre c'est tout'
> meaning 'the man is nothing, the work is everything'

# After reading

## Your personal response

Look back at the story and select five sentences from the text which would sum up what happens. For example your first sentence could be '"Why," says he, "here's another vacancy on the League of Red-Headed Men"' and your last sentence could be '"I could think of nothing save he was running a tunnel to some other building."' Then compare your choices with a partner.

With your partner discuss the questions below.

- What did you like about the story? What didn't you like?
- What question/s would you like to ask Watson?
- What else have you learned about Holmes in this story?

## The role of Watson

It is often said that without Watson there would be no Holmes. What do you think this might mean? In this activity you will be thinking about the importance of Watson in this story.

Read the following extracts. What can you tell about the relationship between Holmes and Watson?

---

### Extract 1

'This gentleman, [Watson] has been my partner and helper in many of my most successful cases, and I have no doubt that he will be of the utmost use to me in yours also.'

---

### Extract 2

'I know, my dear Watson, that you share my love of all that is bizarre and outside the conventions and humdrum routine of everyday life.'

---

### Extract 3

'It is quite a three-pipe problem, and I beg that you won't speak to me for fifty minutes.'

---

### Extract 4

'Evidently,' said I, 'Mr Wilson's assistant counts for a good deal in this mystery of The Red-Headed League. I am sure that you inquired your way merely in order that you might see him.'

'Not him.'

'What then?'

'The knees of his trousers.'

'And what did you see?'

'What I expected to see.'

'Why did you beat the pavement?'

'My dear Doctor, this is a time for observation, not for talk ...'

---

**Extract 5**

I trust that I am not more dense than my neighbours, but I was always oppressed with a sense of my own stupidity in my dealings with Sherlock Holmes. Here I had heard what he had heard, I had seen what he had seen, and yet from his words it was evident that he saw clearly not only what had happened, but what was about to happen, while to me the whole business was still confused and grotesque.

**Extract 6**

'You reasoned it out beautifully,' I exclaimed in unfeigned admiration. 'It is so long a chain, and yet every link rings true.'

Working in groups of three, create a human 'sculpture' to represent the relationship between Holmes and Watson. One member of the group should be the 'artist' who has the final decision about the arrangement of the 'sculpture'. Some groups could show their 'sculpture' to the class. The class should try to guess who is Holmes, and who is Watson, and explain why. The artist can explain his or her 'sculpture' to the class – what have you tried to capture about their relationship?

Think again about the statement 'without Watson there would be no Holmes'. In what ways do you think Holmes might think of Watson as a good friend? In what ways might Holmes find Watson a good assistant in his investigations? Make a note of your ideas.

## Different ways of looking at Watson

You can look at Watson as a character, in other words as a representation of a 'real' person, with thoughts, feelings and emotions. You can also look at Watson as a 'device' in the story. This means that Conan Doyle uses the character of Watson to create certain effects in the reader.

Look again at the extracts above and on page 62 and think about how each one helps the story. You could choose from the statements below or come up with your own ideas.

- This creates tension as Watson, and therefore the reader, does not know what Holmes is thinking.
- The reader is supposed to share Watson's feelings and, as a result, admire Holmes's cleverness as Watson does.
- This gets the reader interested in what might happen next.
- Watson is in the same position as the reader and asks the questions the reader wants to ask.

Discuss what you could now add to your opinions on the statement 'without Watson, there would be no Holmes'. Add to your notes.

## How does Conan Doyle build up tension and create atmosphere?

Re-read the end of the story from 'I placed my revolver, cocked, upon the top of the wooden case behind which I crouched.' to 'In another instant he stood at the side of the hole and was hauling after him a companion, lithe and small like himself, with a pale face and a shock of very red hair.' (Pages 59-60)

Discuss some of the ways in which Doyle builds up tension, for example by emphasising the darkness.

Imagine you are making a television version of 'The Red-Headed League'. Produce a storyboard for this section of the story to show how you would film it. How would you bring out the tension created by Doyle? For example, as John Clay opens up the slab in the floor, you could have an extreme close-up with the camera following the growing gash of light, with only the sound of scraping stone. You could use the format on page 65 to set out your ideas.

## Humour in 'The Red-Headed League'

Here are some of the ways Conan Doyle has created humour in the story:

- Mr Jabez Wilson being a bit slow
- Holmes's reaction to the mystery
- the dialogue between Watson and Holmes
- a ridiculous situation
- the way characters are described
- the way characters behave
- the names of characters
- what characters say.

See if you can find some examples of humour in the story and explain why you find them amusing.

MR JABEZ WILSON

## Storyboard

| | |
|---|---|
| **1** | **2** |
| What you will see on screen | What you will see on screen |
| Sound (music/SFX/dialogue) | Sound (music/SFX/dialogue) |

| | |
|---|---|
| **3** | |
| What you will see on screen | |
| Sound (music/SFX/dialogue) | |

| | |
|---|---|
| **4** | **5** |
| What you will see on screen | What you will see on screen |
| Sound (music/SFX/dialogue) | Sound (music/SFX/dialogue) |

| | |
|---|---|
| **6** | |
| What you will see on screen | |
| Sound (music/SFX/dialogue) | |

# The Speckled Band

## Before reading

### A locked room mystery

'The Speckled Band' is what is sometimes called a 'locked room mystery'. What do you think this might mean?

See if you can solve this locked room mystery (answer on page 128).

**Murder or suicide?**

On a hot summer's day a woman is found hanged in her locked kitchen. There is no sign of anyone having broken into the room or any other signs of struggle. However, there also seems to be nothing that the woman could have stood on to put her head through the noose. There is a puddle of water on the floor. What happened?

### The title

The story is called 'The Speckled Band'. The title comes from a phrase used by Julia Stoner, a woman who dies in the story. She says to her sister, as she is dying, '"Oh my God! Helen! It was the band! The speckled band!"'. With a partner, discuss what you would make of this clue and how you think the 'speckled band' could be involved in Julia's death.

### During reading

As you read the story you will find that at each **PAUSE** symbol there are questions or activities to help you to check your understanding of the story.

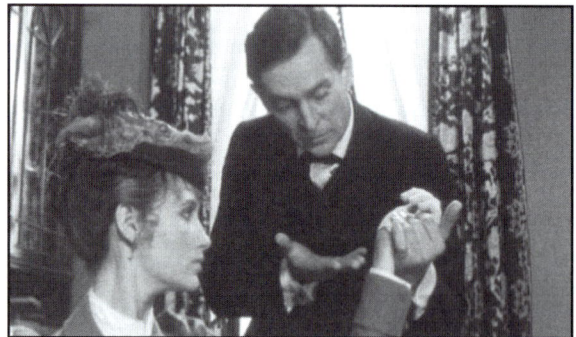

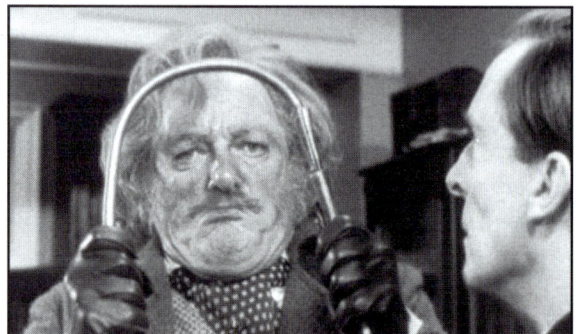

# The Speckled Band

In glancing over my notes of the seventy odd cases in which I have, during the last eight years, studied the methods of my friend, Sherlock Holmes, I find many tragic, some comic, a large number merely strange, but none commonplace; for, working as he did rather for the love of his art than for the acquirement of wealth, he refused to associate himself with any investigation which did not tend towards the unusual, and even the fantastic. Of all these varied cases, however, I cannot recall any which presented more singular features than that which was associated with the well-known Surrey family of the Roylotts of Stoke Moran. The events in question occurred in the early days of my association with Holmes, when we were sharing rooms as bachelors in Baker Street. It is possible that I might have placed them upon record before, but a promise of secrecy was made at the time, from which I have only been freed during the last month by the untimely death of the lady to whom the pledge was given. It is perhaps as well that the facts should now come to light, for I have reason to know that there are widespread rumours as to the death of Dr Grimesby Roylott, which tend to make the matter even more terrible than the truth.

**PAUSE**    **Discuss how Conan Doyle tries to create the impression that there is a real Dr Watson writing a real journal.**

It was early in April, in the year '83, that I woke one morning to find Sherlock Holmes standing, fully dressed, by the side of my bed. He was a late riser, as a rule, and as the clock on the mantelpiece showed me that it was only a quarter-past seven, I blinked up at him in some surprise, and perhaps just a little resentment, for I was myself regular in my habits.

'Very sorry to knock you up, Watson,' said he, 'but it's the common lot this morning. Mrs Hudson has been knocked up, she retorted upon me, and I on you.'

'What is it, then. A fire?'

'No, a client. It seems that a young lady has arrived in a considerable state of excitement, who insists upon seeing me. She is waiting now in the sitting-room. Now, when young ladies wander about the metropolis at this hour of the morning, and knock sleepy people up out of their beds, I presume that it is something very pressing which they have to communicate. Should it prove to be an interesting case, you would, I am sure, wish to follow it from the outset. I thought, at any rate, that I should call you and give you the chance.'

'My dear fellow, I would not miss it for anything.'

I had no keener pleasure than in following Holmes in his professional investigations, and in admiring the rapid deductions, as swift as intuitions, and yet always founded on a logical basis, with which he unravelled the problems which were submitted to him. I rapidly threw on my clothes, and was ready in a few minutes to accompany my friend down to the sitting-room. A lady dressed in black and heavily veiled, who had been sitting in the window, rose as we entered.

'Good-morning, madam,' said Holmes cheerily. 'My name is Sherlock Holmes. This is my intimate friend and associate, Dr Watson, before whom you can speak as freely as before myself. Ha, I am glad to see that Mrs Hudson has had the good sense to light the fire. Pray draw up to it, and I shall order you a cup of hot coffee, for I observe that you are shivering.'

'It is not cold which makes me shiver,' said the woman in a low voice, changing her seat as requested.

'What, then?'

'It is fear, Mr Holmes. It is terror.' She raised her veil as she spoke, and we could see that she was indeed in a pitiable state of agitation, her face all drawn and grey, with restless frightened eyes, like those of some hunted animal. Her features and figure were those of a woman of thirty, but her hair was shot with premature grey, and her expression was weary and haggard. Sherlock Holmes ran her over with one of his quick, all-comprehensive glances.

'You must not fear,' said he soothingly, bending forward and patting her forearm. 'We shall soon set matters right, I have no doubt. You have come in by train this morning, I see.'

'You know me, then?'

'No, but I observe the second half of a return ticket in the palm of your left glove. You must have started early, and yet you had a good drive in a dog-cart, along heavy roads, before you reached the station.'

The lady gave a violent start, and stared in bewilderment at my companion.

'There is no mystery, my dear madam,' said he, smiling. 'The left arm of your jacket is spattered with mud in no less than seven places. The marks are perfectly fresh. There is no vehicle save a dog-cart which throws up mud in that way, and then only when you sit on the left-hand side of the driver.'

'Whatever your reasons may be, you are perfectly correct,' said she. 'I started from home before six, reached Leatherhead at twenty past, and came in by the first train to Waterloo. Sir, I can stand this strain no longer; I shall go mad if it continues. I have no one to turn to – none, save only one, who cares for me, and he, poor fellow, can be of little aid. I have heard of you, Mr Holmes; I have heard of you from Mrs Farintosh, whom you helped in the hour of her sore need. It was from her that I had your address. Oh, sir, do you not think that you could help me, too, and at least throw a little light through the dense darkness which surrounds me? At present it is out of my power to reward you for your services, but in a month or six weeks I shall be married, with the control of my own income, and then at least you shall not find me ungrateful.'

Holmes turned to his desk and, unlocking it, drew out a small case-book, which he consulted.

'Farintosh,' said he. 'Ah yes, I recall the case; it was concerned with an opal tiara. I think it was before your time, Watson. I can only say, madam, that I shall be happy to devote the same care to your case as I did to that of your friend. As to reward, my profession is its reward; but you are at liberty to defray whatever expenses I may be put to, at the time which suits you best. And now I beg that you will lay before us everything that may help us in forming an opinion upon the matter.'

'Alas!' replied our visitor. 'The very horror of my situation lies in the fact that my fears are so vague, and my suspicions depend so entirely upon small points, which might seem trivial to another, that even he to whom of all others I have a right to look for help and advice looks upon all that I tell him about it as the fancies of a nervous woman. He does not say so, but I can read it from his soothing answers and averted eyes. But I have heard, Mr Holmes, that you can see deeply into the manifold wickedness of the human heart. You may advise me how to walk amid the dangers which encompass me.'

'I am all attention, madam.'

'My name is Helen Stoner, and I am living with my stepfather, who is the last survivor of one of the oldest Saxon families in England, the Roylotts of Stoke Moran, on the Western border of Surrey.'

Holmes nodded his head. 'The name is familiar to me,' said he.

'The family was at one time among the richest in England, and the estates extended over the borders into Berkshire in the north, and Hampshire in the west. In the last century, however, four successive heirs were of a dissolute and wasteful disposition, and the family ruin was eventually completed by a gambler in the days of the Regency. Nothing was left save a few acres of ground, and the two-hundred-year-old house, which is itself crushed under a heavy mortgage. The last squire dragged out his existence there, living the horrible life of an aristocratic pauper; but his only son, my stepfather, seeing that he must adapt himself to the new conditions, obtained an advance from a relative, which enabled him to take a medical degree, and went out to Calcutta, where, by his professional skill and his force of character, he established a large practice. In a fit of anger, however, caused by some robberies which had been perpetrated in the house, he beat his native butler to death and narrowly escaped a capital sentence. As it was, he suffered a long term of imprisonment, and afterwards returned to England a morose and disappointed man.

'When Dr Roylott was in India he married my mother, Mrs Stoner, the young widow of Major-General Stoner, of the Bengal Artillery. My sister Julia and I were twins, and we were only two years old at the time of my mother's remarriage. She had a considerable sum of money, not less than a thousand pounds a year, and this she bequeathed to Dr Roylott entirely while we resided with him, with a provision that a certain annual sum should be allowed to each of us in the event of our marriage. Shortly after our return to England my mother died – she was killed eight years ago in a railway accident near Crewe. Dr Roylott then abandoned his attempts to establish himself in practice in London and took us to live with him in the old ancestral house at Stoke Moran. The money which my mother had left was enough for all our wants, and there seemed to be no obstacle to our happiness.

'But a terrible change came over our stepfather about this time. Instead of making friends and exchanging visits with our neighbours, who had at first been overjoyed to see a Roylott of Stoke Moran back in the old family seat, he shut himself up in his house, and seldom came out save to indulge in ferocious quarrels with whoever might cross his path. Violence of temper approaching to mania has been hereditary in the men of the family, and in my stepfather's case it had, I believe, been intensified by his long residence in the tropics. A series of disgraceful brawls took place, two of which ended in the police-court, until at last he became the terror of the village, and the folks would fly at his approach, for he is a man of immense strength, and absolutely uncontrollable in his anger.

'Last week he hurled the local blacksmith over a parapet into a stream and it was only by paying over all the money which I could gather together that I was able to avert another public exposure. He had no friends at all save the wandering gypsies, and he would give these vagabonds leave to encamp upon the few acres of bramble-covered land which represent the family estate, and would accept in return the hospitality of their tents, wandering away with them sometimes for weeks on end. He has a passion also for Indian animals, which are sent over to him by a correspondent, and he has at this moment a cheetah and a baboon, which wander freely over his grounds and are feared by the villagers almost as much as their master.

'You can imagine from what I say that my poor sister Julia and I had no great pleasure in our lives. No servant would stay with us, and for a long time we did all the work of the house. She was but thirty at the time of her death, and yet her hair had already begun to whiten, even as mine has.'

'Your sister is dead, then?'

'She died just two years ago, and it is of her death that I wish to speak to you. You can understand that, living the life which I have described, we were little likely to see anyone of our own age and position. We had, however, an aunt, my mother's maiden sister, Miss Honoria Westphail, who lives near Harrow, and we were occasionally allowed to pay short visits at this lady's house. Julia went there at Christmas two years ago, and met there a half-pay Major of Marines, to whom she became engaged. My stepfather learned of the engagement when my sister returned, and offered no objection to the marriage; but within a fortnight of the day which had been fixed for the wedding, the terrible event occurred which has deprived me of my only companion.'

Sherlock Holmes had been leaning back in his chair with his eyes closed, and his head sunk in a cushion, but he half opened his lids now, and glanced across at his visitor.

'Pray be precise as to details,' said he.

'It is easy for me to be so, for every event of that dreadful time is seared into my memory. The manor house is, as I have already said, very old, and only one wing is now inhabited. The bedrooms in this wing are on the ground floor, the sitting-rooms being in the central block of the buildings. Of these bedrooms the first is Dr Roylott's, the second my sister's, and the third my own. There is no communication between them, but they all open out into the same corridor. Do I make myself plain?'

'Perfectly so.'

'The windows of the three rooms open out upon the lawn. That fatal night Dr Roylott had gone to his room early, though we knew that he had not retired to rest, for my sister was troubled by the smell of the strong Indian cigars which it was his custom to smoke. She left her room, therefore, and came into mine, where she sat for some time, chatting about her approaching wedding. At eleven o'clock she rose to leave me, but she paused at the door and looked back.

'"Tell me, Helen," said she, "have you ever heard anyone whistle in the dead of the night?"

'"Never," said I.

'"I suppose that you could not possibly whistle, yourself, in your sleep?"

'"Certainly not. But why?"

'"Because during the last few nights I have always, about three in the morning, heard a low, clear whistle. I am a light sleeper, and it has awakened me. I cannot tell where it came from; perhaps from the next room, perhaps from the lawn. I thought that I would just ask you whether you had heard it."

'"No, I have not. It must be those wretched gypsies in the plantation."

'"Very likely. And yet if it were on the lawn, I wonder that you did not hear it also."

'"Ah, but I sleep more heavily than you."

'"Well, it is of no great consequence, at any rate." She smiled back at me, closed my door, and a few moments later I heard her key turn in the lock.'

'Indeed,' said Holmes. 'Was it your custom always to lock yourselves in at night?'

'Always.'

'And why?'

'I think that I mentioned to you that the Doctor kept a cheetah and a baboon. We had no feeling of security unless our doors were locked.'

'Quite so. Pray proceed with your statement.'

'I could not sleep that night. A vague feeling of impending misfortune impressed me. My sister and I, you will recollect, were twins, and you know how subtle are the links which bind two souls which are so closely allied. It was a wild night. The wind was howling outside, and the rain was beating and splashing against the windows. Suddenly, amid all the hubbub of the gale, there burst forth the wild scream of a terrified woman. I knew that it was my sister's voice. I sprang from my bed, wrapped a shawl round me, and rushed into the corridor. As I opened my door I seemed to hear a low whistle, such as my sister described, and a few moments later a clanging sound, as if a mass of metal had fallen. As I ran down the passage, my sister's door was unlocked, and revolved slowly upon its hinges. I stared at it horror-stricken, not knowing what was about to issue from it. By the light of the corridor-lamp I saw my sister appear at the opening, her face blanched with terror, her hands groping for help, her whole figure swaying to and fro like that of a drunkard. I ran to her and threw my arms round her, but at that moment her knees seemed to give way and she fell to the ground. She writhed as one who is in terrible pain, and her limbs were dreadfully convulsed. At first I thought that she had not recognized me, but as I bent over her she suddenly shrieked out in a voice which I shall never forget, "Oh, my God! Helen! It was the band! The speckled band!" There was something else which she would fain have said, and she stabbed with her finger into the air in the direction of the Doctor's room, but a fresh convulsion seized her and choked her words. I rushed out, calling loudly for my stepfather, and I met him hastening from his room in his dressing-gown. When he reached my sister's side she was unconscious, and though he poured brandy down her throat and sent for medical aid from the village, all efforts were in vain, for she slowly sank and died without having recovered her consciousness. Such was the dreadful end of my beloved sister.'

'One moment,' said Holmes, 'are you sure about this whistle and metallic sound? Could you swear to it?'

'That was what the county coroner asked me at the inquiry. It is my strong impression that I heard it, and yet, among the crash of the gale and the creaking of an old house, I may possibly have been deceived.'

'Was your sister dressed?'

'No, she was in her night-dress. In her right hand was found the charred stump of a match, and in her left a match-box.'

'Showing that she had struck a light and looked about her when the alarm took place. That is important. And what conclusions did the coroner come to?'

'He investigated the case with great care, for Dr Roylott's conduct had long been notorious in the county, but he was unable to find any satisfactory cause of death. My evidence showed that the door had been fastened upon the inner side, and the windows were blocked by old-fashioned shutters with broad iron bars, which were secured every night. The walls were carefully sounded, and were shown to be quite solid all round, and the flooring was also thoroughly examined, with the same result. The chimney is wide, but is barred up by four large staples. It is certain, therefore, that my sister was quite alone when she met her end. Besides, there were no marks of any violence upon her.'

'How about poison?'

'The doctors examined her for it, but without success.'

'What do you think that this unfortunate lady died of, then?'

'It is my belief that she died of pure fear and nervous shock, though what it was that frightened her I cannot imagine.'

'Were there gypsies in the plantation at the time?'

'Yes, there are nearly always some there.'

'Ah, and what did you gather from this allusion to a band – a speckled band?'

'Sometimes I have thought that it was merely the wild talk of delirium, sometimes that it may have referred to some band of people, perhaps to these very gypsies in the plantation. I do not know whether the spotted handkerchiefs which so many of them wear over their heads might have suggested the strange adjective which she used.'

Holmes shook his head like a man who is far from being satisfied.

**PAUSE**  **Remember the discussion you had before reading the story about what the 'speckled band' might be. Discuss whether you are satisfied with Helen Stoner's suggestions, or whether you have a suggestion of your own.**

'These are very deep waters,' said he; 'pray go on with your narrative.'

'Two years have passed since then, and my life has been until lately lonelier than ever. A month ago, however, a dear friend, whom I have known for many years, has done me the honour to ask my hand in marriage. His name is Armitage – Percy Armitage – the second son of Mr Armitage, of Crane Water, near Reading. My stepfather has offered no opposition to the match, and we are to be married in the course of the spring. Two days ago some repairs were started in the west wing of the building, and my bedroom wall has been pierced, so that I have had to move into the chamber in which my sister died, and to sleep in the very bed in which she slept. Imagine, then, my thrill of terror when last night, as I lay awake, thinking over her terrible fate, I suddenly heard in the silence of the night the low whistle which had been the herald of her own death. I sprang up and lit the lamp, but nothing was to be seen in the room. I was too shaken to go to bed again, however, so I dressed, and as soon as it was daylight I slipped down, got a dog-cart at the Crown Inn, which is opposite, and drove to Leatherhead, from whence I have come on this morning with the one object of seeing you and asking your advice.'

'You have done wisely,' said my friend. 'But have you told me all?'

'Yes, all.'

'Miss Roylott, you have not. You are screening your stepfather.'

'Why, what do you mean?'

For answer Holmes pushed back the frill of black lace which fringed the hand that lay upon our visitor's knee.

Five little livid spots, the marks of four fingers and a thumb, were printed upon the white wrist.

'You have been cruelly used,' said Holmes.

The lady coloured deeply, and covered over her injured wrist. 'He is a hard man,' she said, 'and perhaps he hardly knows his own strength.'

There was a long silence, during which Holmes leaned his chin upon his hands and stared into the crackling fire.

'This is a very deep business,' he said at last. 'There are a thousand details which I should desire to know before I decide upon our course of action. Yet we have not a moment to lose. If we were to come to Stoke Moran today, would it be possible for us to see over these rooms without the knowledge of your stepfather?'

---

**PAUSE**     **Think back to the other stories you have read. How does Holmes's response to Helen Stoner's story differ from his response to Colonel Ross ('Silver Blaze'), the King of Bohemia ('A Scandal in Bohemia'), or Mr Jabez Wilson ('The Red-Headed League')? What is the effect on the reader of the way Holmes responds to Miss Stoner's story?**

---

'As it happens, he spoke of coming into town to-day upon some most important business. It is probable that he will be away all day, and that there would be nothing to disturb you. We have a housekeeper now, but she is old and foolish, and I could easily get her out of the way.'

'Excellent. You are not averse to this trip, Watson?'

'By no means.'

'Then we shall both come. What are you going to do yourself?'

'I have one or two things which I would wish to do now that I am in town. But I shall return by the twelve o'clock train, so as to be there in time for your coming.'

'And you may expect us early in the afternoon. I have myself some small business matters to attend to. Will you not wait and breakfast?'

'No, I must go. My heart is lightened already since I have confided my trouble to you. I shall look forward to seeing you again this afternoon.' She dropped her thick black veil over her face, and glided from the room.

'And what do you think of it all, Watson?' asked Sherlock Holmes, leaning back in his chair.

'It seems to me to be a most dark and sinister business.'

'Dark enough and sinister enough.'

'Yet if the lady is correct in saying that the flooring and walls are sound, and that the door, window, and chimney are impassable, then her sister must have been undoubtedly alone when she met her mysterious end.'

'What becomes, then, of these nocturnal whistles, and what of the very peculiar words of the dying woman?'

'I cannot think.'

'When you combine the ideas of whistles at night, the presence of a band of gypsies who are on intimate terms with this old doctor, the fact that we have every reason to believe that the doctor has an interest in preventing his stepdaughter's marriage, the dying allusion to a band, and, finally, the fact that Miss Helen Stoner heard a metallic clang, which might have been caused by one of those metal bars that secured the shutters falling back into its place, I think that there is good ground to think that the mystery may be cleared along those lines.'

'But what, then, did the gypsies do?'

'I cannot imagine.'

'I see many objections to any such theory.'

'And so do I. It is precisely for that reason that we are going to Stoke Moran this day. I want to see whether the objections are fatal, or if they may be explained away. But what in the name of the devil!'

The ejaculation had been drawn from my companion by the fact that our door had been suddenly dashed open, and that a huge man had framed himself in the aperture. His costume was a peculiar mixture of the professional and of the agricultural, having a black top-hat, a long frock-coat, and a pair of high gaiters, with a hunting-crop swinging in his hand. So tall was he that his hat actually brushed the cross-bar of the doorway, and his breadth seemed to span it across from side to side. A large face, seared with a thousand wrinkles, burned yellow with the sun, and marked with every evil passion, was turned from one to the other of us, while his deep-set, bile-shot eyes, and his high thin fleshless nose, gave him somewhat the resemblance to a fierce old bird of prey.

---

'Which of you is Holmes?' asked this apparition.

'My name, sir, but you have the advantage of me,' said my companion quietly.

'I am Dr Grimesby Roylott, of Stoke Moran.'

'Indeed, Doctor,' said Holmes blandly. 'Pray take a seat.'

'I will do nothing of the kind. My stepdaughter has been here. I have traced her. What has she been saying to you?'

'It is a little cold for the time of the year,' said Holmes.

'What has she been saying to you?' screamed the old man furiously.

'But I have heard that the crocuses promise well,' continued my companion imperturbably.

'Ha! You put me off, do you?' said our new visitor, taking a step forward and shaking his hunting-crop. 'I know you, you scoundrel! I have heard of you before. You are Holmes, the meddler.'

My friend smiled.

'Holmes, the busybody!'

His smile broadened.

'Holmes, the Scotland Yard jack-in-office!'

Holmes chuckled heartily. 'Your conversation is most entertaining,' said he. 'When you go out close the door, for there is a decided draught.'

'I will go when I have had my say. Don't you dare to meddle with my affairs. I know that Miss Stoner has been here – I traced her! I am a dangerous man to fall foul of! See here.' He stepped swiftly forward, seized the poker, and bent it into a curve with his huge brown hands.

'See that you keep yourself out of my grip,' he snarled, and hurling the twisted poker into the fireplace he strode out of the room.

'He seems a very amiable person,' said Holmes, laughing. 'I am not quite so bulky, but if he had remained I might have shown him that my grip was not much more feeble than his own.' As he spoke he picked up the steel poker and, with a sudden effort, straightened it out again.

'Fancy his having the insolence to confound me with the official detective force! This incident gives zest to our investigation, however, and I only trust that our little friend will not suffer from her imprudence in allowing this brute to trace her. And now, Watson, we shall order breakfast, and afterwards I shall walk down to Doctors' Commons, where I hope to get some data which may help us in this matter.'

**PAUSE**     **Talk about what you think of the way Holmes responds to Dr Roylott's threats.**

It was nearly one o'clock when Sherlock Holmes returned from his excursion. He held in his hand a sheet of blue paper, scrawled over with notes and figures.

'I have seen the will of the deceased wife,' said he. 'To determine its exact meaning I have been obliged to work out the present prices of the investments with which it is concerned. The total income, which at the time of the wife's death was little short of £1100 is now, through the fall in agricultural prices, not more than £750. Each daughter can claim an income of £250, in case of marriage. It is evident, therefore, that if both girls had married, this beauty would have had a mere pittance, while even one of them would cripple him to a serious extent. My morning's work has not been wasted, since it has proved that he has the very strongest motives for standing in the way of anything of the sort. And now, Watson, this is too serious for dawdling, especially as the old man is aware that we are interesting ourselves in his affairs; so if you are ready, we shall call a cab and drive to Waterloo. I should be very much obliged if you would slip your revolver into your pocket. An Eley's No. 2 is an excellent argument with gentlemen who can twist steel pokers into knots. That and a toothbrush are, I think, all that we need.'

At Waterloo we were fortunate in catching a train for Leatherhead, where we hired a trap at the station inn, and drove for four or five miles through the lovely Surrey lanes. It was a perfect day, with a bright sun and a few fleecy clouds in the heavens. The trees and wayside hedges were just throwing out their first green shoots, and the air was full of the pleasant smell of the moist earth. To me at least there was a strange contrast between the sweet promise of the spring and this sinister quest upon which we were engaged. My companion sat in the front of the trap, his arms folded, his hat pulled down over his eyes, and his chin sunk upon his breast, buried in the deepest thought. Suddenly, however, he started, tapped me on the shoulder, and pointed over the meadows.

'Look there!' said he.

A heavily timbered park stretched up in a gentle slope, thickening into a grove at the highest point. From amid the branches there jutted out the grey gables and high roof-tree of a very old mansion.

'Stoke Moran?' said he.

'Yes, sir, that be the house of Dr Grimesby Roylott,' remarked the driver.

'There is some building going on there,' said Holmes; 'that is where we are going.'

'There's the village,' said the driver, pointing to a cluster of roofs some distance to the left; 'but if you want to get to the house, you'll find it shorter to get over this stile, and so by the foot-path over the fields. There it is, where the lady is walking.'

'And the lady, I fancy, is Miss Stoner,' observed Holmes, shading his eyes. 'Yes, I think we had better do as you suggest.'

We got off, paid our fare, and the trap rattled back on its way to Leatherhead.

'I thought it as well,' said Holmes as we climbed the stile, 'that this fellow should think we had come here as architects, or on some definite business. It may stop his gossip. Good afternoon, Miss Stoner. You see that we have been as good as our word.'

Our client of the morning had hurried forward to meet us with a face which spoke her joy. 'I have been waiting so eagerly for you,' she cried, shaking hands with us warmly. 'All has turned out splendidly. Dr Roylott has gone to town, and it is unlikely that he will be back before evening.'

'We have had the pleasure of making the Doctor's acquaintance,' said Holmes, and in a few words he sketched out what had occurred. Miss Stoner turned white to the lips as she listened.

'Good heavens!' she cried, 'he has followed me, then.'

'So it appears.'

'He is so cunning that I never know when I am safe from him. What will he say when he returns?'

'He must guard himself, for he may find that there is someone more cunning than himself upon his track. You must lock yourself up from him tonight. If he is violent, we shall take you away to your aunt's at Harrow. Now, we must make the best use of our time, so kindly take us at once to the rooms which we are to examine.'

The building was of grey, lichen-blotched stone, with a high central portion and two curving wings, like the claws of a crab, thrown out on each side. In one of these wings the windows were broken and blocked with wooden boards, while the roof was partly caved in, a picture of ruin. The central portion was in little better repair, but the right-hand block was comparatively modern, and the blinds in the windows, with the blue smoke curling up from the chimneys, showed that this was where the family resided. Some scaffolding had been erected against the end wall, and the stonework had been broken into, but there were no signs of any workmen at the moment of our visit. Holmes walked slowly up and down the ill-trimmed lawn and examined with deep attention the outsides of the windows.

'This, I take it, belongs to the room in which you used to sleep, the centre one to your sister's, and the one next to the main building to Dr Roylott's chamber?'

'Exactly so. But I am now sleeping in the middle one.'

'Pending the alterations, as I understand. By the way, there does not seem to be any very pressing need for repairs at that end wall.'

'There were none. I believe that it was an excuse to move me from my room.'

'Ah! that is suggestive. Now, on the other side of this narrow wing runs the corridor from which these three rooms open. There are windows in it, of course?'

'Yes, but very small ones. Too narrow for anyone to pass through.'

'As you both locked your doors at night, your rooms were unapproachable from that side. Now, would you have the kindness to go into your room and bar your shutters?'

Miss Stoner did so, and Holmes, after a careful examination through the open window, endeavoured in every way to force the shutter open, but without success. There was no slit through which a knife could be passed to raise the bar. Then with his lens he tested the hinges, but they were of solid iron, built firmly into the massive masonry. 'Hum!' said he, scratching his chin in some perplexity, 'my theory certainly presents some difficulties. No one could pass these shutters if they were bolted. Well, we shall see if the inside throws any light upon the matter.'

A small side-door led into the whitewashed corridor from which the three bedrooms opened. Holmes refused to examine the third chamber, so we passed at once to the second, that in which Miss Stoner was now sleeping, and in which her sister had met her fate. It was a homely little room, with a low ceiling and a gaping fireplace, after the fashion of old country-houses. A brown chest of drawers stood in one corner, a narrow white-counter-paned bed in another, and a dressing-table on the left-hand side of the window. These articles, with two small wicker-work chairs, made up all the furniture in the room save for a square of Wilton carpet in the centre. The boards round and the panelling of the walls were of brown, worm-eaten oak, so old and discoloured that it may have dated from the original building of the house. Holmes drew one of the chairs into a corner and sat silent, while his eyes travelled round and round and up and down, taking in every detail of the apartment.

'Where does that bell communicate with?' he asked at last pointing to a thick belt-rope which hung down beside the bed, the tassel actually lying upon the pillow.

'It goes to the housekeeper's room.'

'It looks newer than the other things?'

'Yes, it was only put there a couple of years ago.'

'Your sister asked for it, I suppose?'

'No, I never heard of her using it. We used always to get what we wanted for ourselves.'

'Indeed, it seemed unnecessary to put so nice a bell-pull there. You will excuse me for a few minutes while I satisfy myself as to this floor.' He threw himself down upon his face with his lens in his hand and crawled swiftly backward and forward, examining minutely the cracks between the boards. Then he did the same with the woodwork with which the chamber was panelled. Finally he walked over to the bed and spent some time in staring at it and in running his eye up and down the wall. Finally he took the bell-rope in his hand and gave it a brisk tug.

'Why, it's a dummy,' said he.

'Won't it ring?'

'No, it is not even attached to a wire. This is very interesting. You can see now that it is fastened to a hook just above where the little opening for the ventilator is.'

'How very absurd! I never noticed that before.'

'Very strange!' muttered Holmes, pulling at the rope. 'There are one or two very singular points about this room. For example, what a fool a builder must be to open a ventilator into another room, when, with the same trouble, he might have communicated with the outside air!'

'That is also quite modern,' said the lady.

'Done about the same time as the bell-rope?' remarked Holmes.

'Yes, there were several little changes carried out about that time.'

'They seem to have been of a most interesting character – dummy bell-ropes, and ventilators which do not ventilate. With your permission, Miss Stoner, we shall now carry our researches into the inner apartment.'

Dr Grimesby Roylott's chamber was larger than that of his stepdaughter, but was as plainly furnished. A camp bed, a small wooden shelf full of books, mostly of a technical character, an armchair beside the bed, a plain wooden chair against the wail, a round table, and a large iron safe were the principal things which met the eye. Holmes walked slowly round and examined each and all of them with the keenest interest.

'What's in here?' he asked, tapping the safe.

'My stepfather's business papers.'

'Oh! you have seen inside, then?'

'Only once, some years ago. I remember that it was full of papers.'

'There isn't a cat in it, for example?'

'No. What a strange idea!'

'Well, look at this!' He took up a small saucer of milk which stood on the top of it.

'No; we don't keep a cat. But there is a cheetah and a baboon.'

'Ah, yes, of course! Well, a cheetah is just a big cat, and yet a saucer of milk does not go very far in satisfying its wants, I daresay. There is one point which I should wish to determine.' He squatted down in front of the wooden chair and examined the seat of it with the greatest attention.

'Thank you. That is quite settled,' said he, rising and putting his lens in his pocket. 'Hello! here is something interesting!'

The object which had caught his eye was a small dog lash hung on one corner of the bed. The lash, however, was curled upon itself, and tied so as to make a loop of whipcord.

'What do you make of that, Watson?'

'It's a common enough lash. But I don't know why if should be tied.'

'That is not quite so common, is it? Ah, me! it's a wicked world, and when a clever man turns his brains to crime it is the worst of all. I think that I have seen enough now, Miss Stoner, and, with your permission, we shall walk out upon the lawn.'

I had never seen my friend's face so grim or his brow so dark as it was when we turned from the scene of this investigation. We had walked several times up and down the lawn, neither Miss Stoner nor myself liking to break in upon his thoughts before he roused himself from his reverie.

'It is very essential, Miss Stoner,' said he, 'that you should absolutely follow my advice in every respect.'

'I shall most certainly do so.'

'The matter is too serious for any hesitation. Your life may depend upon your compliance.'

'I assure you that I am in your hands.'

'In the first place, both my friend and I must spend the night in your room.'

Both Miss Stoner and I gazed at him in astonishment.

'Yes, it must be so. Let me explain. I believe that that is the village inn over there?'

'Yes, that is the 'Crown'.'

'Very good. Your windows would be visible from there?'

'Certainly.'

'You must confine yourself to your room, on pretence of a headache, when your stepfather comes back. Then when you hear him retire for the night, you must open the shutters of your window, undo the hasp, put your lamp there as a signal to us, and then withdraw quietly with everything which you are likely to want into the room which you used to occupy. I have no doubt that, in spite of the repairs, you could manage there for one night.'

'Oh, yes, easily.'

'The rest you will leave in our hands.'

'But what will you do?'

'We shall spend the night in your room, and we shall investigate the cause of this noise which has disturbed you.'

'I believe, Mr Holmes, that you have already made up your mind,' said Miss Stoner, laying her hand upon my companion's sleeve.

'Perhaps I have.'

'Then, for pity's sake, tell me what was the cause of my sister's death.'

'I should prefer to have clearer proofs before I speak.'

'You can at least tell me whether my own thought is correct, and if she died from some sudden fright.'

'No, I do not think so. I think that there was probably some more tangible cause. And now, Miss Stoner, we must leave you, for if Dr Roylott returned and saw us, our journey would be in vain. Good-bye, and be brave, for if you will do what I have told you, you may rest assured that we shall soon drive away the dangers that threaten you.'

Sherlock Holmes and I had no difficulty in engaging a bedroom and sitting-room at the Crown Inn. They were on the upper floor, and from our window we could command a view of the avenue gate, and of the inhabited wing of Stoke Moran Manor House. At dusk we saw Dr Grimesby Roylott drive past, his huge form looming up beside the little figure of the lad who drove him. The boy had some slight difficulty in undoing the heavy iron gates, and we heard the hoarse roar of the Doctor's voice and saw the fury with which he shook his clinched fists at him. The trap drove on, and a few minutes later we saw a sudden light spring up among the trees as the lamp was lit in one of the sitting-rooms.

'Do you know, Watson,' said Holmes as we sat together in the gathering darkness, 'I have really some scruples as to taking you tonight. There is a distinct element of danger.'

'Can I be of assistance?'

'Your presence might be invaluable.'

'Then I shall certainly come.'

'It is very kind of you.'

'You speak of danger. You have evidently seen more in these rooms than was visible to me.'

'No, but I fancy that I may have deduced a little more. I imagine that you saw all that I did.'

'I saw nothing remarkable save the bell-rope, and what purpose that could answer I confess is more than I can imagine.'

'You saw the ventilator, too?'

'Yes, but I do not think that it is such a very unusual thing to have a small opening between two rooms. It was so small that a rat could hardly pass through.'

'I knew that we should find a ventilator before ever we came to Stoke Moran.'

'My dear Holmes!'

'Oh, yes, I did. You remember in her statement she said that her sister could smell Dr Roylott's cigar. Now, of course that suggests at once that there must be a communication between the two rooms. It could only be a small one, or it would have been remarked upon at the coroner's inquiry. I deduced a ventilator.'

'But what harm can there be in that?'

'Well, there is at least a curious coincidence of dates. A ventilator is made, a cord is hung, and a lady who sleeps in the bed dies. Does not that strike you?'

'I cannot as yet see any connection.'

'Did you observe anything very peculiar about that bed?'

'No.'

'It was clamped to the floor. Did you ever see a bed fastened like that before?'

'I cannot say that I have.'

'The lady could not move her bed. It must always be in the same relative position to the ventilator and to the rope – or so we may call it, since it was clearly never meant for a bell-pull.'

'Holmes,' I cried, 'I seem to see dimly what you are hinting at. We are only just in time to prevent some subtle and horrible crime.'

'Subtle enough and horrible enough. When a doctor does go wrong he is the first of criminals. He has nerve and he has knowledge. Palmer and Pritchard were among the heads of their profession. This man strikes even deeper, but, I think, Watson, that we shall be able to strike deeper still. But we shall have horrors enough before the night is over; for goodness' sake let us have a quiet pipe, and turn our minds for a few hours to something more cheerful.'

**PAUSE**    **Discuss what you make of the clues given so far. What are your theories about the case?**

About nine o'clock the light among the trees was extinguished, and all was dark in the direction of the Manor House. Two hours passed slowly away, and then, suddenly, just at the stroke of eleven, a single bright light shone out right in front of us.

'That is our signal,' said Holmes, springing to his feet; 'it comes from the middle window.'

As we passed out he exchanged a few words with the landlord, explaining that we were going on a late visit to an acquaintance, and that it was possible that we might spend the night there. A moment later we were out on the dark road, a chill wind blowing in our faces, and one yellow light twinkling in front of us through the gloom to guide us on our sombre errand.

There was little difficulty in entering the grounds, for unrepaired breaches gaped in the old park wall. Making our way among the trees, we reached the lawn, crossed it, and were about to enter through the window, when out from a clump of laurel bushes there darted what seemed to be a hideous and distorted child, who threw itself on the grass with writhing limbs, and then ran swiftly across the lawn into the darkness.

'My God!' I whispered; 'did you see it?'

Holmes was for the moment as startled as I. His hand closed like a vice upon my wrist in his agitation. Then he broke into a low laugh, and put his lips to my ear.

'It is a nice household,' he murmured. 'That is the baboon.'

I had forgotten the strange pets which the doctor affected. There was a cheetah, too; perhaps we might find it upon our shoulders at any moment. I confess that I felt easier in my mind when, after following Holmes's example and slipping off my shoes, I found myself inside the bedroom. My companion noiselessly closed the shutters, moved the lamp onto the table, and cast his eyes round the room. All was as we had seen it in the day-time. Then creeping up to me and making a trumpet of his hand, he whispered into my ear again so gently that it was all that I could do to distinguish the words:

'The least sound would be fatal to our plans.'

I nodded to show that I had heard.

'We must sit without light. He would see it through the ventilator.'

I nodded again.

'Do not go to sleep; your very life may depend upon it. Have your pistol ready in case we should need it. I will sit on the side of the bed, and you in that chair.'

I took out my revolver and laid it on the corner of the table.

Holmes had brought up a long thin cane, and this he placed upon the bed beside him. By it he laid the box of matches and the stump of a candle. Then he turned down the lamp, and we were left in darkness.

How shall I ever forget that dreadful vigil? I could not hear a sound, not even the drawing of a breath, and yet I knew that my companion sat open-eyed, within a few feet of me, in the same state of nervous tension in which I was myself. The shutters cut off the least ray of light, and we waited in absolute darkness. From outside came the occasional cry of a nightbird, and once at our very window a long drawn, cat-like whine, which told us that the cheetah was indeed at liberty. Far away we could hear the deep tones of the parish clock, which boomed out every quarter of an hour. How long they seemed, those quarters! Twelve struck, and one and two and three, and still we sat waiting silently for whatever might befall.

**PAUSE**     **Discuss how Conan Doyle builds tension in this section. How does his use of language, for example the length of sentences and paragraphs, heighten the effect?**

Suddenly there was the momentary gleam of a light up in the direction of the ventilator, which vanished immediately, but was succeeded by a strong smell of burning oil and heated metal. Someone in the next room had lit a dark lantern. I heard a gentle sound of movement, and then all was silent once more, though the smell grew stronger. For half an hour I sat with straining ears. Then suddenly another sound became audible – a very gentle, soothing sound, like that of a small jet of steam escaping continually from a kettle. The instant that we heard it, Holmes sprang from the bed, struck a match, and lashed furiously with his cane at the bell-pull.

'You see it, Watson?' he yelled. 'You see it?'

But I saw nothing. At the moment when Holmes struck the light I heard a low, clear whistle, but the sudden glare flashing into my weary eyes made it impossible for me to tell what it was at which my friend lashed so savagely. I could, however, see that his face was deadly pale and filled with horror and loathing.

He had ceased to strike, and was gazing up at the ventilator, when suddenly there broke from the silence of the night the most horrible cry to which I have ever listened. It swelled up louder and louder, a hoarse yell of pain and fear and anger all mingled in the one dreadful shriek. They say that away down in the village, and even in the distant parsonage, that cry raised the sleepers from their beds. It struck cold to our hearts, and I stood gazing at Holmes, and he at me, until the last echoes of it had died away into the silence from which it rose.

'What can it mean?' I gasped.

'It means that it is all over,' Holmes answered. 'And perhaps, after all, it is for the best. Take your pistol, and we will enter Dr Roylott's room.'

With a grave face he lit the lamp and led the way down the corridor. Twice he struck at the chamber door without any reply from within. Then he turned the handle and entered, I at his heels, with the cocked pistol in my hand.

It was a singular sight which met our eyes. On the table stood a dark-lantern with the shutter half open, throwing a brilliant beam of light upon the iron safe, the door of which was ajar. Beside this table, on the wooden chair, sat Dr Grimesby Roylott, clad in a long grey dressing-gown, his bare ankles protruding beneath, and his feet thrust into red heelless Turkish slippers. Across his lap lay the short stock with the long lash which we had noticed during the day. His chin was cocked upwards, and his eyes were fixed in a dreadful, rigid stare at the corner of the ceiling. Round his brow he had a peculiar yellow band, with brownish speckles, which seemed to be bound tightly round his head. As we entered he made neither sound nor motion.

'The band! the speckled band!' whispered Holmes.

I took a step forward: in an instant his strange headgear began to move, and there reared itself from among his hair the squat diamond-shaped head and puffed neck of a loathsome serpent.

'It is a swamp adder!' cried Holmes; 'the deadliest snake in India. He has died within ten seconds of being bitten. Violence does, in truth, recoil upon the violent, and the schemer falls into the pit which he digs for another. Let us thrust this creature back into its den, and we can then remove Miss Stoner to some place of shelter and let the county police know what has happened.'

As he spoke he drew the dog-whip swiftly from the dead man's lap, and throwing the noose round the reptile's neck he drew it from its horrid perch and, carrying it at arm's length, threw it into the iron safe, which he closed upon it.

Such are the true facts of the death of Dr Grimesby Roylott, of Stoke Moran. It is not necessary that I should prolong a narrative which has already run to too great a length, by telling how we broke the sad news to the terrified girl, how we conveyed her by the morning train to the care of her good aunt at Harrow, of how the slow process of official inquiry came to the conclusion that the Doctor met his fate while indiscreetly playing with a dangerous pet. The little which I had yet to learn of the case was told me by Sherlock Holmes as we travelled back next day.

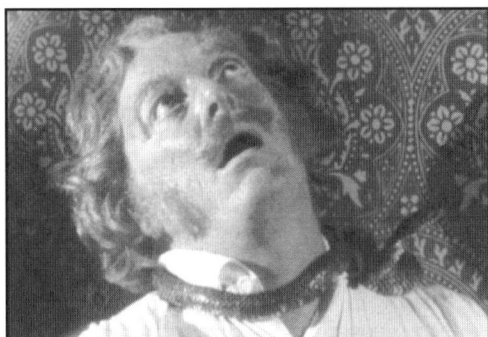

'I had,' said he, 'come to an entirely erroneous conclusion which shows, my dear Watson, how dangerous it always is to reason from insufficient data. The presence of the gypsies, and the use of the word 'band,' which was used by the poor girl, no doubt to explain the appearance which she had caught a hurried glimpse of by the light of her match, were sufficient to put me upon an entirely wrong scent. I can only claim the merit that I instantly reconsidered my position when, however, it became clear to me that whatever danger threatened an occupant of the room could not come either from the window or the door. My attention was speedily drawn, as I have already remarked to you, to this ventilator, and to the bell-rope which hung down to the bed. The discovery that this was a dummy, and that the bed was clamped to the floor, instantly gave rise to the suspicion that the rope was there as a bridge for something passing through the hole, and coming to the bed. The idea of a snake instantly occurred to me, and when I coupled it with my knowledge that the doctor was furnished with a supply of creatures from India, I felt that I was probably on the right track. The idea of using a form of poison which could not possibly be discovered by any chemical test was just such a one as would occur to a clever and ruthless man who had had an Eastern training. The rapidity with which such a poison would take effect would also, from his point of view, be an advantage. It would be a sharp-eyed coroner, indeed, who could distinguish the two little dark punctures which would show where the poison fangs had done their work. Then I thought of the whistle. Of course he must recall the snake before the morning light revealed it to the victim. He had trained it, probably by the use of the milk which we saw, to return to him when summoned. He would put it through this ventilator at the hour that he thought best, with the certainty that it would crawl down the rope and land on the bed. It might or might not bite the occupant, perhaps she might escape every night for a week, but sooner or later she must fall a victim.

'I had come to these conclusions before ever I had entered his room. An inspection of his chair showed me that he had been in the habit of standing on it, which of course, would be necessary in order that he should reach the ventilator. The sight of the safe, the saucer of milk, and the loop of whipcord were enough to finally dispel any doubts which may have remained. The metallic clang heard by Miss Stoner was obviously caused by her stepfather hastily closing the door of his safe upon its terrible occupant. Having once made up my mind, you know the steps which I took in order to put the matter to the proof. I heard the creature hiss as I have no doubt that you did also, and I instantly lit the light and attacked it.'

'With the result of driving it through the ventilator.'

'And also with the result of causing it to turn upon its master at the other side. Some of the blows of my cane came home and roused its snakish temper, so that it flew upon the first person it saw. In this way I am no doubt indirectly responsible for Dr Grimesby Roylott's death, and I cannot say that it is likely to weigh very heavily upon my conscience.'

# After reading

## A locked room mystery

Remind yourself of the locked room mystery you tried to solve before reading 'The Speckled Band' (page 66).

Re-write the central puzzle of 'The Speckled Band' as a brief locked room mystery (using no more than 150 words). Swap your version with a partner and help each other to check that you have included all the essential clues. Try out your puzzle on friends or family who have not read the story. Can they solve the mystery? What do they think of the solution?

HE MADE NEITHER SOUND NOR MOTION

## Your personal response – tracing tension in the story

One way to trace your response to the build up of suspense and tension in a story is to map it on a chart.

On a copy of the chart on page 80, trace the tension in 'The Speckled Band' by putting a small X to show how far up the tension scale you would rate each event in the story. Then join all your Xs together to make a continuous line to show the pattern of tension. What do you notice?

Compare your chart with someone else's and discuss similarities and differences.

You could try doing a tension chart for the other stories you have read and compare patterns. Which story did you find the most tense? Does the way tension builds up in each story follow a similar pattern?

Studying Sherlock Holmes **79**

# A tension graph

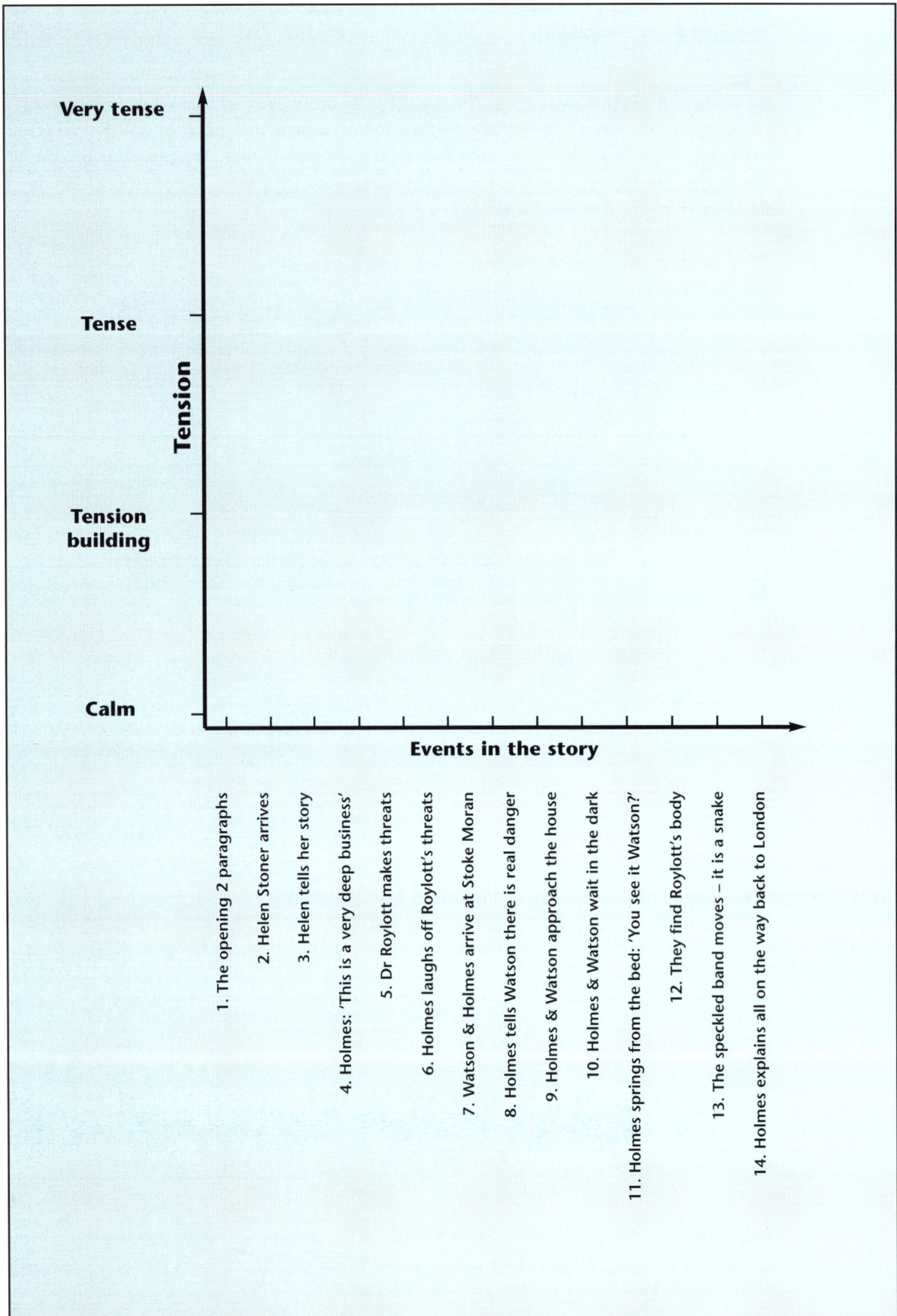

Tension

**Very tense**

**Tense**

**Tension building**

**Calm**

Events in the story

1. The opening 2 paragraphs
2. Helen Stoner arrives
3. Helen tells her story
4. Holmes: 'This is a very deep business'
5. Dr Roylott makes threats
6. Holmes laughs off Roylott's threats
7. Watson & Holmes arrive at Stoke Moran
8. Holmes tells Watson there is real danger
9. Holmes & Watson approach the house
10. Holmes & Watson wait in the dark
11. Holmes springs from the bed: 'You see it Watson?'
12. They find Roylott's body
13. The speckled band moves – it is a snake
14. Holmes explains all on the way back to London

## Holmes's sense of justice – an opinion continuum

In crime stories the detective is the hero, fighting on the side of good. Often the detective needs their own strong sense of justice: they may have to do things alone if the legal system is corrupt or incompetent; they may even have to bend the law in order to get the right result in the end. Sherlock Holmes is a private detective, which gives him more freedom than the police officer who must do everything within the law. He is often shown to have his own sense of justice.

**Label one wall of your classroom 'strongly agree' and the opposite wall 'strongly disagree'. Imagine a line running between the two opposites, representing the range of possible opinions between 'strongly agree' and 'strongly disagree'. This is an 'opinion continuum'.**

**For each example below, decide whether you think Holmes is right or whether he is just arrogant in thinking he is above the law.**

**As your teacher reads out an example, move to a position on the continuum (the imaginary line) to show how far you agree or disagree with Holmes's sense of justice – the closer you are to the 'strongly agree' wall, the more you agree with Holmes's actions, and so on.**

**Once everyone has taken up their position, the teacher could ask one or two people to explain their view, and to try to persuade others to move closer to their position.**

---

### From 'Silver Blaze'

When Holmes finds Silver Blaze at Capelton stables, he decides to make a deal with Silas Brown, the owner of the stables who had found the horse and decided to keep him. In return for his treating the horse well and running it in the race, Holmes promises to tell no-one where the horse was kept. He says he is doing this partly because he thinks Brown deserves mercy and will not get it from Colonel Ross. However, he also says he wants to tease the Colonel by running the horse in disguise as revenge for the Colonel's being disrespectful to him. He tells Watson:

'I follow my own methods and tell as much or as little as I choose. That is the advantage of being unofficial.'

---

### From 'A Scandal in Bohemia'

Holmes tricks his way into Irene Adler's home by impersonating a priest. He explains his plan to Watson:

'You don't mind breaking the law?'

'Not in the least!'

'Nor running the chance of arrest?'

'Not in a good cause.'

'Oh, the cause is excellent!'

---

> **From 'The Speckled Band'**
>
> **Holmes feels he may be partly responsible for Dr Roylott's snake turning on him and killing him:**
>
> '... Some of the blows of my cane came home and roused its snakish temper, so that it flew upon the first person it saw. In this way I am no doubt indirectly responsible for Dr Grimesby Roylott's death, and I cannot say that it is likely to weigh very heavily upon my conscience.'

**Finally, thinking about the stories overall, move to a position on the continuum to show your opinion on the statement 'Holmes has a good sense of justice'.**

## One of the best Holmes stories?

Various groups of people, from readers of *The Strand Magazine* (where the Holmes stories originally appeared) to societies of Sherlock Holmes fans, have voted 'The Speckled Band' their favourite story. Conan Doyle himself included it in the top twelve of his own favourite Holmes stories.

**With a partner, discuss why you think 'The Speckled Band' is such a popular story. You might want to consider some of the points which follow.**

- The characters of Holmes and Watson – how they appear in the story and the relationship between them.
- Conan Doyle's use of language.
- How tension is built up.
- How Doyle creates atmosphere and uses setting.
- The puzzle of the crime.
- The unusual solution.
- The fact that the story is about a murder.

**Find evidence from the story for five of your key points and present them to another pair.**

Other people have criticised the story for having a ridiculous solution: for a man who prided himself on having created a 'scientific detective', Conan Doyle makes a number of howling errors to make the story work, such as those listed below.

- Snakes can't climb ropes, don't drink milk and are deaf (so couldn't hear a 'low whistle').
- There's no such thing as an Indian swamp adder.
- No snake is poisonous enough to kill a fully grown adult in a few seconds.

**With a partner, discuss whether these inaccuracies make any difference to your enjoyment of the story. Obviously it will make a difference whether or not you already knew any of these facts when you first read the story. Compare your views with others in the class.**

**Which story in this collection have you most enjoyed? Why? Again, compare your opinion with others in the class.**

# After reading

## Character

### The character of Sherlock Holmes

**How realistic is Sherlock Holmes?**

> **In a small group, make a list of words to describe Holmes's personality and the features that make him a good detective. If you did the 'Before reading' activity on pages 6-9, the notes you made then will help you.**

In *Just the Facts Ma'am: a writer's guide to investigators and investigation techniques*, Greg Fallis (himself an experienced real-life private detective) explains some of the characteristics a real-life detective needs to be successful.

> **Which of these qualities, shown in the box on page 84, does Sherlock Holmes have?**

**10. Physically fit**

A detective never knows when s/he might have to chase a suspect or climb a tree to spy on someone.

**1. Intense curiosity**

A desire to know and to understand will motivate the detective to investigate thoroughly and solve the crime.

**2. Street sense**

The detective needs to be able to survive on the street and be aware of what is happening around them.

**9. Professional distance**

A detective can't afford to get too emotionally involved in a case. Good detectives learn how to control the powerful emotions a crime might evoke, such as pity, fear or disgust. They need to be able to do this in order to look at the evidence objectively.

**3. Able to fit in anywhere and get on with anyone**

Investigating a crime involves getting information from people. If the detective can put someone at ease, they are more likely to talk. The detective should not be easily intimidated by a person's status or rank – they must be determined to get information from anyone.

# An ideal detective?

**8. Good listener**

Again, important for getting information from people. The detective shouldn't interrupt with jokes, demands, or more and more questions.

**4. Determination**

Solving a crime may be hard work. It may involve revealing people's secrets or telling them things they don't really want to know. The detective needs determination.

**7. Problem solving ability**

Detectives have to be good at solving puzzles and problems. They have to be able to take information that may seem unconnected and work out how it all fits together.

**6. A strong sense of self**

In order to get information, or solve a case, a detective may have to do things which might go against their usual values, or which might seem wrong to people outside the case. The detective therefore needs to know inside when they are doing the right thing for the right reasons.

**5. A fund of diverse information**

A detective never knows what sort of information might be useful. Knowing a little about all sorts of things will also help them to get on with lots of different people.

## The role of the hero

Fictional detectives have to hold the interest of the reader, not just be realistic. If crime stories are all about the fight of good against evil, then it is the detective who is the hero.

**Read these two quotations from well-known crime writers about the qualities a fictional detective needs.**

**With a partner, try to answer the questions below.**

- What do these writers think are the essential characteristics for the hero/detective? Add any you hadn't thought of to your own list of features.
- How many of these features does Holmes have? Draw a chart like the one below.

> But down these mean streets a man must go who is not himself mean, who is neither tarnished nor afraid. The detective in this kind of story must be such a man. He is the hero; he is everything. He must be a complete man and a common man and yet an unusual man. He must be, to use a rather weathered phrase, a man of honour – by instinct, by inevitability, without thought of it, and certainly without saying it. He must be the best man in his world, and a good enough man in any world ... He is a lonely man and his pride is that you will treat him as a proud man or be very sorry you ever saw him ... The story is this man's adventure in search of a hidden truth.
>
> **Raymond Chandler, *The Simple Art of Murder***

> I write about the deeds of the fallen. The killers. The chaos. The disorder. With one good man – the investigator – I then restore order. I take the box of jumbled puzzle pieces and make the picture whole. That is what the mystery is all about. Not the solution to the puzzle but the act of putting the pieces together. There is a difference. It may be subtle but it is there. And in that difference is the reason we love mystery novels. They reassure us. They tell us that indeed the puzzle can be carefully constructed and put back together, that order can always be restored, that chaos does not win the day.
>
> This act of reassurance cannot take place without a noble man or woman at the centre of the story. A person unafraid to wade into that which we don't want to know about and find the solution that will vanquish evil and restore order.
>
> **Michael Connolly, 'The Mystery Of Mystery Writing', published in the *Walden Book Report***

| Characteristics of a hero | Is Holmes like this? | Evidence to back up my opinion |
|---|---|---|
|  |  |  |
|  |  |  |
|  |  |  |
|  |  |  |
|  |  |  |
|  |  |  |

# The character of Watson

Remind yourself of the work you did on Watson in the after reading activities on 'The Red-Headed League' (pages 62-63).

## Different representations of Watson

In several of the television and film adaptations of Sherlock Holmes stories, Watson is presented as a slow, bumbling idiot. Many fans of the stories complain that this is not an accurate representation of Watson in the stories, and that Watson only seems slow because of Holmes's brilliance.

**If you have watched any film or television versions, you could think about how Watson was played. Otherwise, you could look at the images below, and on page 87, from different productions, and talk about what impressions they give of Watson's character.**

**Working with a partner, one of you should work to find evidence in the stories you have read to show that Watson is a slow, bumbling idiot, and the other that he is simply ordinarily intelligent.**

**When you have finished, compare evidence and decide how you view Watson.**

**Imagine you were casting a television version of the story. What sort of actor would you choose to play Watson? What instructions would you give them about how to play the part?**

Watson on left

Watson on left

Watson on right

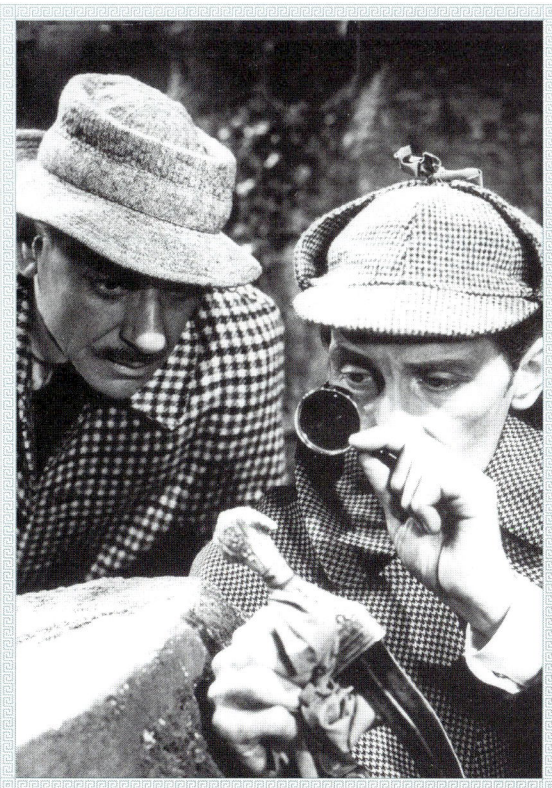

Watson on left

Watson on left

# Structure

## The structure of the crime story

One of the reasons for the incredible success of the Sherlock Holmes stories is that they offer both familiarity (knowing what to expect, identifying regular characters, familiar plot structure and so on) *and* variety (unusual characters and intriguing mysteries). Soap operas and sitcoms are very popular on television for similar reasons.

**Look at the ingredients of a typical Sherlock Holmes story on page 89. Make a chart like the one below with a column for each story you have read. Start with your first story and pick out the ingredients which have been included. List the ingredients on your chart in the order in which they appear in the story. Then move on to another story.**

| 'Silver Blaze' | 'The Red-Headed League' | 'The Speckled Band' |
|---|---|---|
| 1. A crime | 1. Someone comes to see Holmes and explain their problem. | 1. Someone comes to see Holmes and explain their problem. |
| 2. A false trail | | |
| 3. Holmes explores the scene | | |
| | | |
| | | |
| | | |

**When you have finished your chart discuss the questions below.**

• What do the stories have in common?
• How does Conan Doyle create variety?

# Ingredients of a Sherlock Holmes story

A false trail: a wrongly accused suspect or a clue that leads in the wrong direction.

A helpless victim.

A clever villain.

A crime or an attempted crime.

Holmes explains the solution to Watson.

Holmes admits he has made a mistake.

Others have tried to solve the case and failed.

Someone comes to see Holmes and explain their problem.

Holmes seems to have worked out the solution but no-one else has.

A victim the reader feels sympathetic towards.

You, the reader, work out the solution.

Holmes questions witnesses or explores the crime scene and seems to have discovered something important, but the reader (and Watson) isn't sure what, or isn't sure of the significance of what he has found.

## How does he do it? Sherlock Holmes's methods

Another important aspect of the way the stories are structured is the way Conan Doyle reveals information about the case. Dr Watson, and therefore the reader, is given most of the same information as Sherlock Holmes and yet Holmes usually solves the case first. How does he do this?

### How to be a good detective

**For each of the following extracts make a note in your own words about the methods Holmes uses to solve cases.**

---

**From 'A Scandal in Bohemia'**

'You see, but you do not observe. The distinction is clear. For example, you have frequently seen the steps which lead up from the hall to this room.'

'Frequently'...

'Then how many are there?'

'How many! I don't know.'

'Quite so! You have not observed. And yet you have seen.'

---

**From 'A Case of Identity'**

'Never trust to general impressions, my boy, but concentrate yourself upon the details.'

---

**From 'Silver Blaze'**

'See the value of imagination ... we imagined what might have happened, acted upon the supposition, and find ourselves justified.'

---

**From 'A Scandal in Bohemia'**

'It is a capital mistake to theorise before one has data. Insensibly one begins to twist facts to suit theories, instead of theories to suit facts.'

---

**From 'The Beryl Coronet'**

'It is an old maxim of mine that when you have excluded the impossible, whatever remains, however improbable, must be the truth.'

---

**From 'Silver Blaze'**

'One true inference invariably suggests others.'

---

All these quotations refer to Holmes's famous logic. However, there is another important method that he often uses, as the quotations on page 91 reveal.

**From 'Silver Blaze'**

We all sprang out with the exception of Holmes, who continued to lean back with his eyes fixed upon the sky in front of him, entirely absorbed in his own thoughts ...

'Excuse me,' said he '... I was day dreaming'. There was a gleam in his eye and a suppressed excitement in his manner which convinced me, used as I was to his ways, that his hand was upon a clue, though I could not imagine where he had found it.

**From 'The Man With the Twisted Lip'**

'... I am sure, Mr Holmes, that we are very much indebted to you for having cleared the matter up. I wish I knew how you reach your results.'

'I reached this one,' said my friend, 'by sitting upon five pillows and consuming an ounce of shag [tobacco].'

You may have noticed yourself that sometimes thinking really hard about a problem is not the best way to solve it. If you let your mind drift, think about something else for a while, or even have a good night's sleep, sometimes the answer just comes to you. It seems as though another part of your mind, which some people call your unconscious mind, has been working away to find a solution.

# How does he do it? Conan Doyle's methods

Of course, Sherlock Holmes doesn't solve the case before the reader just because he (or rather Conan Doyle) is more intelligent – it's all in the way the stories are structured.

In his autobiography, *Memories and Adventures*, Conan Doyle describes how he plots a Sherlock Holmes story:

> The first thing is to get your idea. Having got that key idea one's next task is to conceal it and lay emphasis on everything which can make for a different explanation.

Quite often in a Holmes story, as in 'Silver Blaze', the police already have a suspect and all the clues seem to be pointing towards them. Only Sherlock Holmes sees the holes and problems in the police case.

Of course, the stories are presented as if they have been written by Dr Watson, and Holmes sometimes refers to the way Watson 'cheats' the reader. In 'The Crooked Man' Holmes says when Watson writes the stories of their adventures he makes them effective by 'retaining in your own hands some factors in the problem which are never imparted to the reader.'

**What do you think he means? Can you think of an example from one of the stories you have read?**

## How clues are hidden

If Conan Doyle simply cheated and left out important clues so that only Holmes knew about them, readers would soon get frustrated with the stories. Instead he gives information gradually so that the reader feels as if he or she is working alongside Holmes and has the same clues that he has. However, tiny but important fragments of the clues are kept from the reader. In 'Silver Blaze', you may remember, Holmes asks the Inspector for a photograph of John Straker, but he does not tell us what he is going to do with it, or what he discovers as a result.

Another technique Conan Doyle uses is to hide a clue by overloading the reader with information.

**Read this extract from 'The Red-Headed League.' Can you remember what vital clue was hidden in this paragraph? (You can check by looking back at page 61.)**

> 'Let me see,' said Holmes, standing at the corner and glancing along the line, 'I should like just to remember the order of the houses here. It is a hobby of mine to have an exact knowledge of London. There is Mortimer's, the tobacconist, the little newspaper shop, the Coburg branch of the City and Suburban Bank, the Vegetarian Restaurant, and McFarlane's carriage-building depot. That carries us right on to the other block. And now, Doctor, we've done our work, so it's time we had some play. A sandwich and a cup of coffee, and then off to violin-land, where all is sweetness and delicacy and harmony, and there are no red-headed clients to vex us with their conundrums.'

# Point of view

## Different narrators

Read the following extracts. Who is telling the story in each one?

> **Version 1**
>
> Holmes stood outside the police cell, seemingly lost in thought. Perhaps he was contemplating the fate of the criminal inside, but I knew he would not waste much time on that subject for his quick mind was always onto the new. He leaned towards me and said 'Fried eggs for breakfast Watson?'
>
> 'How the devil did you know that?' I exclaimed.

> **Version 2**
>
> Inside the cell the prisoner was curled up on the narrow bed, wondering what would become of him now. Holmes stood outside, apparently lost in thought. He smiled slightly and then seemed to bring himself back to reality. Suddenly he took a keen interest in the front of Watson's coat. 'Fried eggs for breakfast Watson?' he said.
>
> 'How the devil did you know that?' the good doctor exclaimed.

> **Version 3**
>
> I stood outside the police cell and allowed myself a moment of self-congratulation at the thought of another cunning criminal sitting behind bars where he belonged. It was not long before my mind had leapt to another topic however, for my thoughts are always searching for a new mystery to solve. Just at that moment the mystery occupying my thoughts was the origin of that stain on Watson's coat. I peered a little closer. It was definitely egg yolk. I leaned towards him and said, 'Fried eggs for breakfast Watson?'
>
> 'How the devil did you know that?' my good companion exclaimed.

In doing this activity you have been thinking about the 'narrator', the imaginary person who seems to be telling the story. The narrator can be one of the characters in the story, the author themselves or an observer. The way the narrator is related to the imaginary world of the story is called the **'point of view'**.

Version 1 is written in the **first person** from the **point of view** of Dr Watson (like the Holmes stories). Version 2 is written as if someone outside the story were observing and describing without bringing in their own opinions or personality. It is written from the **third person** point of view, in other words there is no 'I' to tell the story. Version 3 is from Holmes's point of view. It is also written from the **first person** point of view, but in this version it is written as if Holmes himself were speaking to the reader.

Take a short section from one of the stories you have been reading. With a partner, re-write it from a third person perspective (like Version 2) and then from the point of view of Holmes (like Version 3).

**Now look back at the original. Discuss the questions listed below.**

- Which version makes you more sympathetic towards Holmes?
- Which version makes you more sympathetic to Watson?
- Which makes you admire Holmes more?
- Which makes Holmes seem more realistic?
- Which makes Holmes seem more perfect?
- Which creates more mystery and suspense?

**Read the two extracts below in which a crime fiction reader and a crime fiction writer talk about different narrative points of view.**

---

### Mark Bernstein

When mystery writers choose the first person, they usually employ it to highlight the limits of the protagonist* – to emphasize the weakness of the individual in the face of great and malicious forces. Hard-boiled writers like Dashiell Hammett and Sarah Paretsky use the first person to emphasize how feeble and limited their heroes are. Despite their physical prowess, we are always aware how little their heroes know, how vulnerable they feel, and how great is the personal cost of the resolution they achieve.

*Protagonist=hero*

---

### John Morgan Wilson, author of the 'Simple Justice' series

I tried writing for years in the third person, and found it constricting and artificial; it never worked for me. The moment I wrote the first line of *Simple Justice* in the first person, using the pronoun 'I', I found my narrative voice, and just kept writing. It seemed to put me in touch with my emotions and memories, and the writing really flowed. It felt more honest and real, almost as if I was talking to the reader. However, after four *Justice* novels, I've just finished a thriller in the third person, writing different chapters from different ('multiple') viewpoints. It was a nice change, though difficult until I got the hang of it. That omniscient*, third person perspective gives you a lot of advantages over the first person – with the third person, the (invisible) narrator can literally be anywhere, inside any character's head and heart, all-knowing and all-seeing. In the first person, you are limited in some ways; you must always be where your narrator is, seeing and knowing only what the narrator does. I'd recommend experimenting with different viewpoints, to find what works best for you, or suits the material.

*Omniscient=all-knowing*

---

## 'Sherlock Holmes is made possible by Watson'

It is often said that 'without Watson, there would be no Holmes'. What do you think this might mean? If you did the activities after reading 'The Red-Headed League' (see pages 62-63), remind yourself of the work you did. If not, turn to page 62 and do the activity on 'The Role of Watson'.

**Discuss why you think Conan Doyle chose to write the stories in the first person from Watson's point of view.**

# Style

## Conan Doyle's style – dialogue

### Balance of description and dialogue

Pick three pages at random from each story and, each time you do, estimate what percentage of the page is dialogue, what percentage is description and what percentage is narration (telling the plot). Look carefully – sometimes the whole page is someone speaking so you need to check whether there are speech marks at the beginning of each paragraph to show a very long section of speech.

Why do you think Conan Doyle uses so much dialogue? Use the questions below to get you started.

- How does he try to keep the pace of the story going?
- How does he put clues across?
- How does the dialogue often become a story within the story – either told to Holmes or by Holmes?

### The relationship between Holmes and Watson

What do you learn about the relationship between Watson and Holmes through their speech?

Look at the examples below and on page 96 of dialogue between Holmes and Watson talking, re-written as a script. Read each one aloud with a partner and then do the activities that follow on pages 96 and 97.

---

**From 'The Red-Headed League'**

| | |
|---|---|
| **Watson:** | I am sure you inquired your way merely in order that you might see him. |
| **Holmes:** | Not him. |
| **Watson:** | What then? |
| **Holmes:** | The knees of his trousers. |
| **Watson:** | And what did you see? |
| **Holmes:** | What I expected to see. |
| **Watson:** | Why did you beat the pavement? |
| **Holmes:** | My dear Doctor, this is a time for observation, not for talk ... We know something of Saxe-Coburg Square. Let us now explore the paths which lie behind it. |

---

**From 'Silver Blaze'**

**Watson:** But what then did the gypsies do?

**Holmes:** I have no idea.

**Watson:** I see many objections to any such theory.

**Holmes:** And so do I. It is precisely for that reason that we are going to Stoke Moran this day.

---

**From 'Silver Blaze'**

**Watson:** Tuesday evening! And this is Thursday morning. Why did you not go down yesterday?

**Holmes:** Because I made a blunder, my dear Watson – which is, I am afraid to say, a more common occurrence than anyone would think who only knew me through your memoirs ... yet in some ways I feel that yesterday has not been wasted.

**Watson:** You have formed a theory then?

**Holmes:** At least I have a grip of the essential facts of the case. I shall enumerate them to you, for nothing clears up a case so much as stating it to another person, and I can hardly expect your co-operation if I do not show you the position from which we start.

---

Draw a chart like the one below to show the number of different sentence types used by Holmes and by Watson and then answer the questions on page 97.

| Sentence type | Number used by Watson | Number used by Holmes |
|---|---|---|
| Statements | | |
| Questions | | |
| Commands | | |
| Exclamations | | |

What does this show about Watson and about Holmes? What does it tell you about the relationship between them? How is the reader helped by the fact that Watson asks lots of questions?

What else can you tell from their dialogue, for example, about the way people spoke at this time?

With a partner, write a short piece of dialogue between Holmes and Watson, using Conan Doyle's style as much as possible. When you have finished, read it aloud to see if it sounds right.

You could now look back at the dialogue in one of the stories you have been reading to see what else you can tell from the way people speak. For example, you could see if there are any differences between the ways women and men speak or the ways people of different classes speak.

# The stories in context

## Crime fiction

### A short history of crime fiction

#### The beginnings

Crimes have been written about for centuries, but it was in the 17th Century, with the growth of journalism, that writing about crime became really popular in England. In the late 17th Century criminals were executed by public hanging and these executions were spectator events, drawing large crowds. Early journalists would rush out 'broadsheets' (like a one sheet newspaper) which told the (often not very accurate) tale of the life and crimes of the person being executed. Broadsheets would also tell the stories of criminals who became popular heroes by, for example, escaping several times, and people would follow the fortunes of their favourites, looking forward to reading about their latest crime or arrest.

#### Eugène François Vidocq

The police force was also becoming more professional and well-organised. Robert Peel set up the first Metropolitan Police (for London) in 1829, and by 1860 there were the beginnings of a modern police force in Britain. This helped the development of crime writing, as there were more records and more systematic investigations, although the main role of the police was seen as preventing crime, rather than detecting it.

In France there was an extraordinary man called Eugène François Vidocq. He had started as a criminal, then became a police informer, and eventually became director of the 'Sûreté' – a newly started professional police force in France. Among other things he was the first to make plaster casts of foot and shoe impressions, he introduced a card-index system for proper record keeping, and introduced the police force to ballistics (how to work out from bullet holes and other evidence what happened in a shooting). Vidocq was a master of disguise and surveillance. After leaving the Sûreté he set up the first private investigation agency. Vidocq published his memoirs and his ghost-writer (the person who helped him write his memoirs down) made sure he came across as a superbly intelligent policeman outwitting an assortment of evil criminals. A real hero in fact! Conan Doyle used quite a few elements of Vidocq in creating the character of Holmes.

### Edgar Allen Poe

Edgar Allen Poe was well-known for his crime stories in the 19th Century and his stories are still popular today. Although he can't really be called the inventor of the detective story he certainly created a certain kind of detective. Poe drew a little from Vidocq's memoirs and created Chevalier C Auguste Dupin, a brilliant detective. The character of Dupin was of a highly intelligent gentleman crime-solver who is rather isolated from society. He tackles crimes that the police have been unable to solve. Does this sound a bit like Sherlock Holmes? Doyle was a great admirer of the Poe stories (even though he has Holmes say in *A Study in Scarlet*, 'In my opinion, Dupin was a very inferior sort of fellow').

### Clue-Puzzle Stories

Sherlock Holmes, created by Sir Arthur Conan Doyle, had his own 'scientific method' based on the awareness of the importance of every tiny detail. In Doyle's stories the reader (and Dr Watson) is caught by surprise when a detail only Holmes has noticed or understood turns out to be the key to solving a complex mystery. This kind of story became known as the 'clue-puzzle' detective story. One of the most popular writers of this kind of story was Agatha Christie who wrote an incredible number of novels in the 1930s. She created two famous detectives: the very English Miss Marple and the Belgian Hercule Poirot who, like Holmes, had a companion (Captain Hastings) to whom he explained some, but not all, of his thinking.

The clue-puzzle style of detective story focuses on a logical puzzle which can only be solved by looking at the clues in the right way. This kind of story invites the reader to work alongside the detective as he/she solves the puzzle. Sometimes the reader can solve the puzzle before the detective, sometimes the reader finds that they have been fooled by the author all along.

### Crime Fiction Today

From the days of Poe, through the Sherlock Holmes stories, the detective is nearly always a member of the upper middle class or even an aristocrat, extremely intelligent and often a little eccentric. Modern writers of crime fiction in English have created detectives from all walks of life, from different cultures and backgrounds. These days the police force is much bigger, better organised and more advanced than in Doyle's day, with access to computer records and scientific techniques that would not be available to the private investigator or amateur. As a result there has also been a growth in fiction about the professionals: police detectives; forensics experts; pathologists and criminal profilers. There is an amazing variety within the genre (see pages 126-127 for some further reading suggestions) but most readers of crime fiction still have some admiration for Sherlock Holmes and his creator Sir Arthur Conan Doyle.

## Why do people read crime fiction?

Below and on page 101 you will find some opinions about why people read crime fiction, or watch films or television programmes about crime.

**Read the statements. Can you add any ideas of your own?**

**Put the statements, including any of your own, in rank order with the one you agree with most as number one, to show why you think people read crime fiction, or watch films and television programmes about crime.**

**Now pick out the three statements which best describe what you *personally* have enjoyed about the Sherlock Holmes stories. Again, compare your opinions with others in the class. Do people seem to be enjoying the stories for the same reasons, or are their reasons very different?**

**Now discuss why you think the Sherlock Holmes stories have been so popular for such a long time, using the work you have done in this section to inform the discussion.**

> ■ Detective fiction really engages the reader because you have to pay close attention to the characters and the plot in order to try to solve the crime before the author solves it for the reader. A good detective story makes you feel you are part of the action.

> ■ The detective story makes it possible to experience excitement, passion, and danger, but in a safe way.

> ■ Crime fiction is basically about good fighting evil, and we like to know that good will win in the end.

> ■ Detective stories are like crossword puzzles. You have to look at the clues in the right way to solve the mystery and, if you do, you feel immense satisfaction. People like a detective story that makes them feel as if they are working alongside the detective to solve the crime.

> ■ Crime happens in every society and in all walks of life – it affects everyone, so crime fiction is a genre that can appeal to everyone.

■ Because crime fiction deals with all the little details of every day life it is a great way to find out about people in different times and places.

■ Crime fiction might seem to be about crime, about finding the solution to the puzzle, but actually it is about the efforts of the hero and the process of putting the pieces of the puzzle together. It is this process that the reader likes because it reassures them that order can be restored, that things can be put right. Everyone experiences chaos and difficulty in their lives – that's why we like to be reassured that chaos does not win the day.

■ We like crime fiction because it shows us the dark side of life, and that always fascinates people.

■ It's all about suspense and tension – people like to be on the edge of their seats.

■ In many ways, crime fiction gives adults what children take from fairy tales: the reassurance that comes from seeing your worst fears acted out in the suffering of imaginary victims, whose tormentors are ultimately punished.

■ Fairy tales may end with those wonderfully familiar words, 'and they all lived happily ever after', but these days a large number of adult crime novels have open endings, in which it is very clear that some criminals will escape and few victims or investigators can expect unalloyed happiness. While that takes something away from the reassurance, it makes what is left more convincing because the stories themselves are more realistic. (Natasha Cooper – crime fiction writer)

# Class and status

In the Sherlock Holmes stories Conan Doyle believed he had shown Holmes to be mainly interested in the case, and to have little interest in for someone's status in society. The following drama activity will help you to think about Holmes's (and probably Conan Doyle's) attitudes to class and status.

Your teacher will give you a role card from the selection below and on page 103.

**Look at your card but don't reveal it to anyone else. Read the quotations from the stories and think about how Holmes behaved towards your character. How much respect did he have for your character? Did your character have a lot of respect for Holmes?**

**Now read *all* the role cards to remind yourself about each character (but still do not reveal which character you have been given).**

**Turn to page 104 to find out what to do next.**

---

## Colonel Ross

### 'Silver Blaze'

'Colonel Ross still wore an expression which showed the poor opinion which he had formed of my companion's ability.'

**Holmes says to Watson:**
'… the Colonel's manner has been just a trifle cavalier to me. I'm inclined to have a little amusement at his expense.'

**The Colonel to Holmes after the mystery is solved:**
'My dear sir, you have done wonders.'

**Holmes to the Colonel at the end:**
'If you care to smoke a cigar in our rooms, Colonel, I shall be happy to give you any further details which might interest you.'

### High Status

---

## Mr Jabez Wilson

### 'The Red-Headed League'

**Holmes asks:**
'Perhaps, Mr Wilson, you would have the great kindness to recommence your narrative?'

'If you can do nothing better than laugh at me, I can go elsewhere.'
'No, no' cried Holmes, shoving him back in the chair from which he had half risen.

### Low Status

An 'Average British tradesman'

---

## John Clay

### 'The Red Headed League'

'John Clay, the murderer, thief, smasher, and forger.'

**Holmes says:**
'He is a remarkable man is young John Clay. His grandfather was a royal duke, and he himself has been to Eton and Oxford.'

**John Clay to Sherlock Holmes:**
'…You seem to have done the thing very completely. I must compliment you.'
'And I you,' Holmes answered. 'Your Red-Headed idea was very new and effective.'

**John Clay to the police man:**
'I beg that you will not touch me with your filthy hands … I have royal blood in my veins.'

### High and low status

**Educated, aristocratic, but criminal**

## Irene Adler

### 'A Scandal in Bohemia'

**Watson about Holmes:**
… for Holmes she is always *the* woman. He (Holmes) used to make merry over the cleverness of women, but I have not heard him do it of late.

**Irene Adler in her letter to Holmes:**
'You really did it very well. You took me in completely.'

### Low Status

**Former opera singer**

## The King

### 'A Scandal in Bohemia'

**Holmes to the King:**
Holmes laughed. 'It is quite a pretty little problem,' said he.
'But a very serious one to me,' returned the King reproachfully.

**Holmes to the King:**
'From what I have seen of the lady she seems indeed to be on a very different level to your majesty,' said Holmes coldly.

**Holmes to the King:**
'I have the honour to wish you good morning.' He bowed and, turning away without observing the hand which the King had stretched out to him, he set off in my company for his chambers.

### Very High Status

## Helen Stoner

### 'The Speckled Band'

**Holmes to Miss Stoner:**
'These are very deep waters … Pray go on with your narrative.'

**Holmes to Watson about Miss Stoner:**
'I only trust that our little friend will not suffer from her imprudence in allowing this brute to trace her.'

**Holmes to Miss Stoner:**
'Goodbye, and be brave, for if you do what I have told you, you may rest assured that we shall soon drive away the dangers that threaten you.'

### High Status

**Upper middle class**

You will need to clear some space in the classroom. Your teacher will then ask someone to come and act the part of Holmes and one other person to come and act the part of the character on their role card. The other character should show their role card to Sherlock Holmes *but* the two of them should not have any discussion, nor should the role card be shown to anyone else.

**Imagine that the two characters are walking along the pavement in Victorian London from opposite directions. The pavement is narrow, the road is busy. In the middle of the pavement, between the two characters, is a deep puddle so that there is only room for one person to get past. They certainly don't want to step into the road – in Victorian times the road would have been full of horse manure! As the two characters approach the puddle, they must decide what they are going to do.**

- They recognise each other: will they greet each other? If so, how? Who will give way at the puddle? How will each behave towards the other?
- The two characters act out this scene, without revealing the character's name.
- The audience try to guess which character met Holmes at the puddle.
- Once the character has been revealed, discuss the scene. Did the way the characters behave fit the way you saw them in the story?

## Who gets respect from Holmes?

**Now re-read all the role cards. Discuss who you think gets respect from Holmes and why. You could use the statements below to start your discussion.**

- Holmes doesn't respect anyone. He just thinks he is superior to everyone else.
- Holmes doesn't care about someone's class or status in society, he treats everyone the same.
- It might seem as if Holmes doesn't care about class or status, but he is much more patronising or rude to working class people than people of the same class as he is (or higher).
- Holmes only respects those who are as intelligent as he is.
- Holmes respects others who are good at what they do.
- Holmes doesn't respect those who have got their position through birth or luck, rather than through hard work.
- Like many men of the time, Holmes tends to be polite to women, but patronising.

# Crime and criminals

Attitudes towards criminals changed during the Victorian era. At the beginning of the 19th Century people believed that criminals were simply lazy members of the working class who preferred a life of crime and idleness to doing an honest day's work. By Doyle's time criminals were considered to be suffering from some sort of behavioural abnormality, either inherited or caused by bad parenting or a breakdown in family life.

**Read the statements below and on page 106 about attitudes towards crime and criminals.**

**Choose the three you agree with most strongly. Compare your choices with a partner.**

- Criminals are people forced by circumstances into a certain way of life, for example through being poor and not having any other way of making enough money for the life-style they want to lead.

- Some people are just evil and always will be.

- Almost everyone has broken the law at some point – we've all avoided paying the fare on the bus, pretended we were old enough to get into a certain film, bought cigarettes under age, kept the money when a shopkeeper gave us too much change or something like that – so we're all criminals really.

- Just because someone commits a crime it doesn't make them a criminal for life. People can change with help and the right circumstances.

- People who commit crimes tend to have had a difficult upbringing.

- People choose to be criminals because it is an easy way to make money.

- There's a difference between those involved in petty crime, like burglars, and those who commit serious crimes, like murders.

- You don't know what you might do in difficult circumstances, for example a battered wife might be pushed to the limit and kill her husband, but not be a danger to anyone else.

Newgate prison

■ It doesn't matter *why* someone has committed a crime. They might have a good reason, but that doesn't excuse what they have done.

■ Sometimes you have to break the law to do the right thing – the law can't cover every possibility. Most people know, deep down, whether something is morally right or wrong.

■ Saying what is right and what is wrong is not as simple as it seems. People have had different ideas about what is right and wrong at different times and in different cultures and religions. The law can only represent one way of looking at right and wrong.

**What would you add if you were to make your own statement? Collect together some different additional statements from the whole class.**

**Does Conan Doyle seem to put across particular opinions about crime through the stories? Look again at the statements above and at your own statement/s. What attitudes to crime do you notice in the stories? Choose the three statements you think Sherlock Holmes would agree with most strongly and find evidence for them from the stories.**

# Sir Arthur Conan Doyle fact file

■ Arthur Doyle was born in Edinburgh, Scotland, on 22nd May 1859.

■ He graduated from Edinburgh University with a degree in medicine in 1881. One of his professors was Dr Joseph Bell, an expert in using careful observation to diagnose disease. The Doctor showed Conan Doyle how to make deductions about patients by observing them closely, for example to tell what they did for a living. Bell was to be to be one of the models for Sherlock Holmes.

■ His first short story (not a detective story) was published in 1879.

■ He practised (not very successfully) as a doctor from 1882-1891.

- In 1887 he published *A Study in Scarlet,* the first short novel featuring Sherlock Holmes and Dr Watson.

- In 1890 *The Strand Magazine* was founded and published a series of short stories – 'The Adventures of Sherlock Holmes'. Both the magazine and the detective became extremely popular.

- Conan Doyle also wrote historical novels, science fiction and serious articles. He was knighted for his non-fiction writing on the Boer War.

- He was so worried that he would only be remembered for the 'lesser work' of the Sherlock Holmes stories that he tried to kill off the great detective in a story called 'The Final Problem'. However, there was such a public outcry that he felt obliged to bring Holmes back to life. Of course, he was right about being remembered only for Sherlock Holmes – these days few people read his other novels or non-fiction books, although he wrote many.

- Conan Doyle solved the real-life case of George Edalji, wrongly accused of mutilating animals and killing a horse in Staffordshire. Doyle investigated the case, showed the mistakes made by the police, and found the real culprit. The public outcry caused by his work in this case was one of the factors which led to the creation of the Court of Appeal.

- At one time the Chinese and the Egyptian police recommended Conan Doyle's works as training textbooks. J Edgar Hoover, chief of the FBI declared that they had incorporated all Holmes's methods and the French Sûreté named a criminal laboratory after him.

- Conan Doyle died in 1930 having been married twice and fathered five children.

- If you search for 'Sherlock Holmes' on the Internet you will get over 500,000 references in many different languages.

- Even today, the Post Office receives letters for Mr Sherlock Holmes of 221b Baker Street, asking for help in clearing the name of a wrongly accused person.

# Coursework assignments

## Meeting the criteria

This section offers you help with writing a coursework assignment on Sherlock Holmes. Pages 110-118 offer advice on planning, structuring and writing an assignment. Some suggested assignment titles are given on pages 119-125.

The chart on page 110 is designed to help you to meet the coursework criteria. The 'extension' questions will help you if you are hoping to get above a 'C'. However, you will need to talk to your teacher about the specific criteria for the specification you are following.

# Meeting the coursework criteria

| | |
|---|---|
| **Writer's use of language** | You could comment on: the balance of dialogue, description and narration (telling the story); descriptive techniques; the way characters speak to each other (including different types of sentences). Remember to explain the effect of the techniques on the reader. |
| **Extension** | How is the writer's use of language affected by the time and place in which he is writing? |
| **Characters and situations** | Did you feel you were working alongside the detective to solve the crime? What did you think about Dr Watson? Is Holmes a typical hero? Why/why not? What were your opinions about different characters at different points in the stories – did they change? |
| **Extension** | Think about the characters as devices in the story. For example, how does Watson work as a plot device? How does the character of Holmes reflect society's attitudes at the time the stories were written? |
| **Structure** | Look again at the opening of two stories – how does Conan Doyle try to draw you in? How does he structure the stories to give the readers some variety and some familiar elements? Does he give you all the information you need to solve the mystery? Why? |
| **Extension** | How does Conan Doyle create suspense? (For example through the use of Watson as the narrator.) Give an example of the way clues build up through the story. |
| **Social, historical, cultural context** | When and where were the stories set? How do you think this affects the writer's use of language or the way he has presented characters or events in the story (for example the 'scandal' in 'A Scandal in Bohemia')? It might help to think about how the story might be different if it were set in a different time or place. What kind of detective stories are these? Why do you think people enjoy reading this kind of story? |
| **Personal response** | What did you enjoy? What did you dislike in the stories? Explain why. |
| **Extension** | Think about one or two points in the stories where another reader might have interpreted it differently (for example, why Holmes fails in 'A Scandal in Bohemia'). It will be helpful to remember class and small group discussions where different people expressed different views. Where might a Victorian reader have reacted differently (for example to the way women, men, working class people or different races are portrayed)? |

# Writing a critical essay

## Structuring your essay

An essay needs:

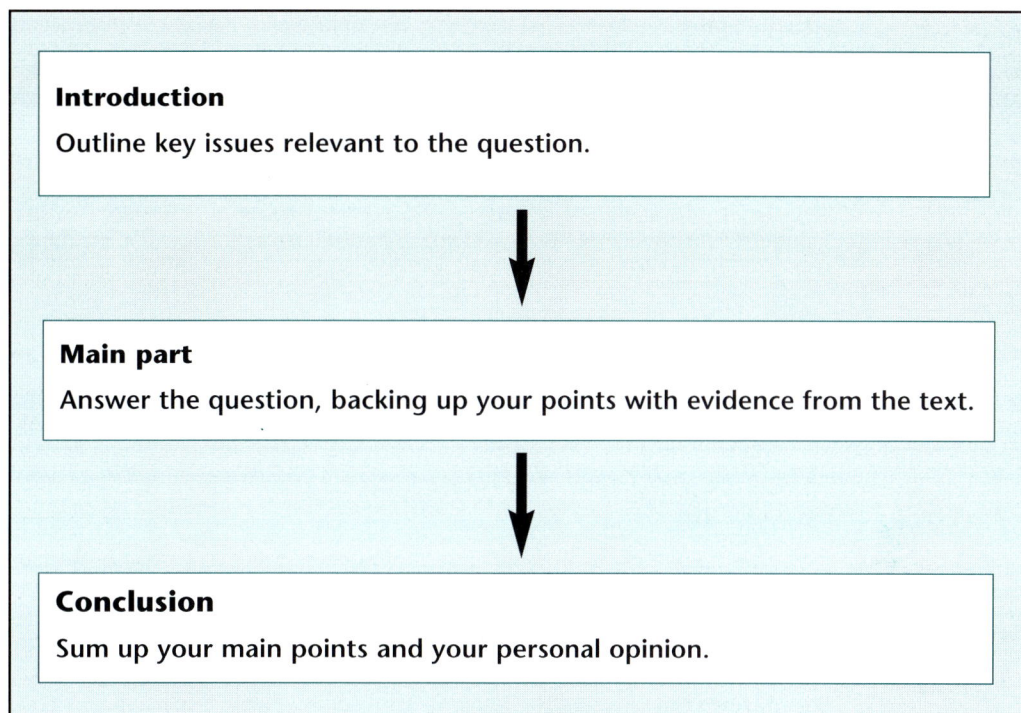

**Introduction**
Outline key issues relevant to the question.

↓

**Main part**
Answer the question, backing up your points with evidence from the text.

↓

**Conclusion**
Sum up your main points and your personal opinion.

You are now going to look in more detail at how to structure paragraphs within the essay.

## Structuring a paragraph

As a general rule each paragraph should contain the following:
• a statement of a point that answers the question
• a quotation or example from the text that supports your point
• some sort of comment or explanation to go with the evidence
• a development of your ideas.

One way to remember this is with the mnemonic 'SEED'.

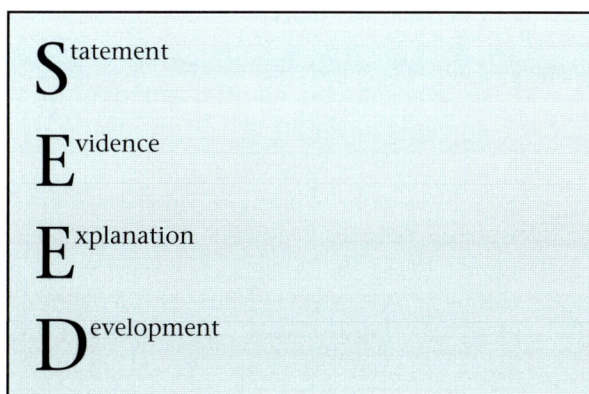

**S**tatement

**E**vidence

**E**xplanation

**D**evelopment

However, you can change the order of the ingredients.

Here are some examples of paragraphs from essays about Sherlock Holmes.

**With a partner, read the paragraphs and try to identify:**

- the statement, evidence, explanation and development
- what the writer has done to develop the idea in the point, for example: taking a point further; expressing a personal opinion; discussing other possible interpretations.

**Example paragraph 1**

One way in which Holmes is a typical detective is that he seems to be isolated. In 'A Scandal in Bohemia' Watson says Holmes 'loathed every form of society' and from this, and the fact that we never meet any other friends of Holmes in the stories, it seems that Watson is Holmes's only friend. I think that Holmes's aloneness (it is difficult to know if he is 'lonely') makes him seem even more unique to the reader. Readers might also feel a bit sorry for him, which prevents him from seeming so super-human that you can't relate to him at all.

**Example paragraph 2**

'To Sherlock Holmes she is always *the* woman.' This is the opening sentence of 'A Scandal in Bohemia'. It is obvious, right from the beginning of the story with the use of italics for 'the', that this woman is special, even though Watson insists that 'It was not that he (Holmes) felt any emotion akin to love for Irene Adler'. The opening of the story is a hint or a warning that this time Holmes's usual brilliance is going to fail him. It is almost as if Conan Doyle thought that the idea of Holmes failing would be so shocking that he needed to prepare the reader.

# Using quotations

The way you use quotations makes a big difference to how sophisticated your essay sounds.

**Read the two paragraphs above again and this time notice how a quotation can be used as part of your sentence (for instance, ... even though Watson insists that 'It was not that he (Holmes) felt any emotion akin to love for Irene Adler' ...). This avoids having to keep introducing each quotation with 'for example'.**

**What has the writer done with the quotation in each paragraph? For example: an explanation of how the evidence supports the point; a comment on the writer's use of language in the quotation; an explanation of the effect on the reader.**

# Making comparisons

The way you make comparisons between the stories will make a difference to the grade you get. Here are some ways to improve the way you manage comparisons.

## Structuring your essay

When you are writing a comparative essay the simplest way to structure it is like this:

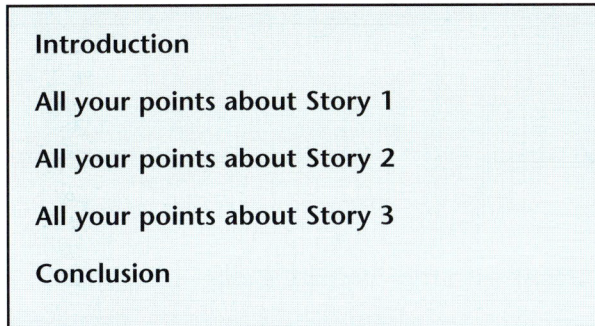

> **Introduction**
>
> **All your points about Story 1**
>
> **All your points about Story 2**
>
> **All your points about Story 3**
>
> **Conclusion**

However, this makes it very difficult for you to make comparisons across the stories and is not likely to get you the highest marks. Below and on page 114 are two other ways you could structure your essay:

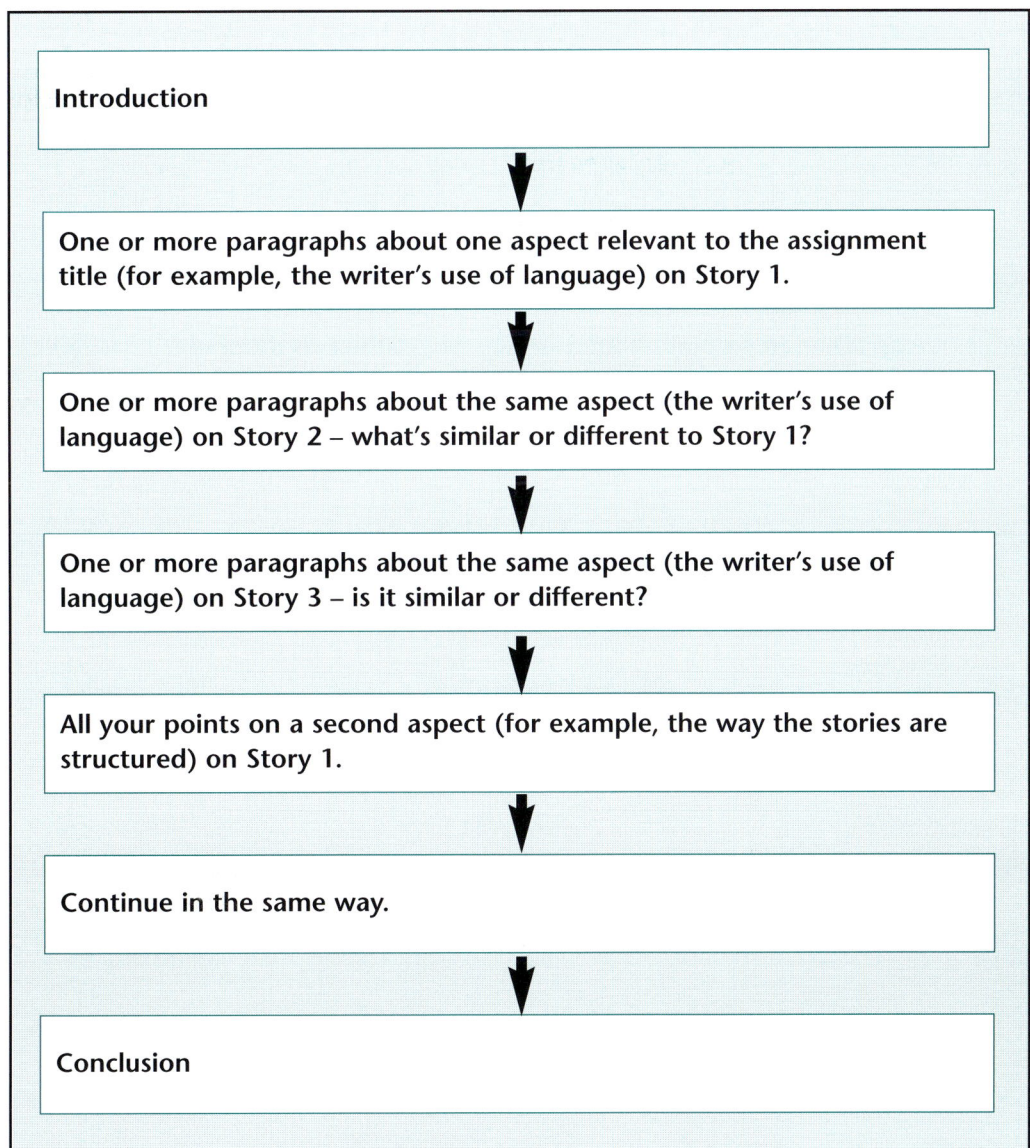

> **Introduction**
>
> ↓
>
> **One or more paragraphs about one aspect relevant to the assignment title (for example, the writer's use of language) on Story 1.**
>
> ↓
>
> **One or more paragraphs about the same aspect (the writer's use of language) on Story 2 – what's similar or different to Story 1?**
>
> ↓
>
> **One or more paragraphs about the same aspect (the writer's use of language) on Story 3 – is it similar or different?**
>
> ↓
>
> **All your points on a second aspect (for example, the way the stories are structured) on Story 1.**
>
> ↓
>
> **Continue in the same way.**
>
> ↓
>
> **Conclusion**

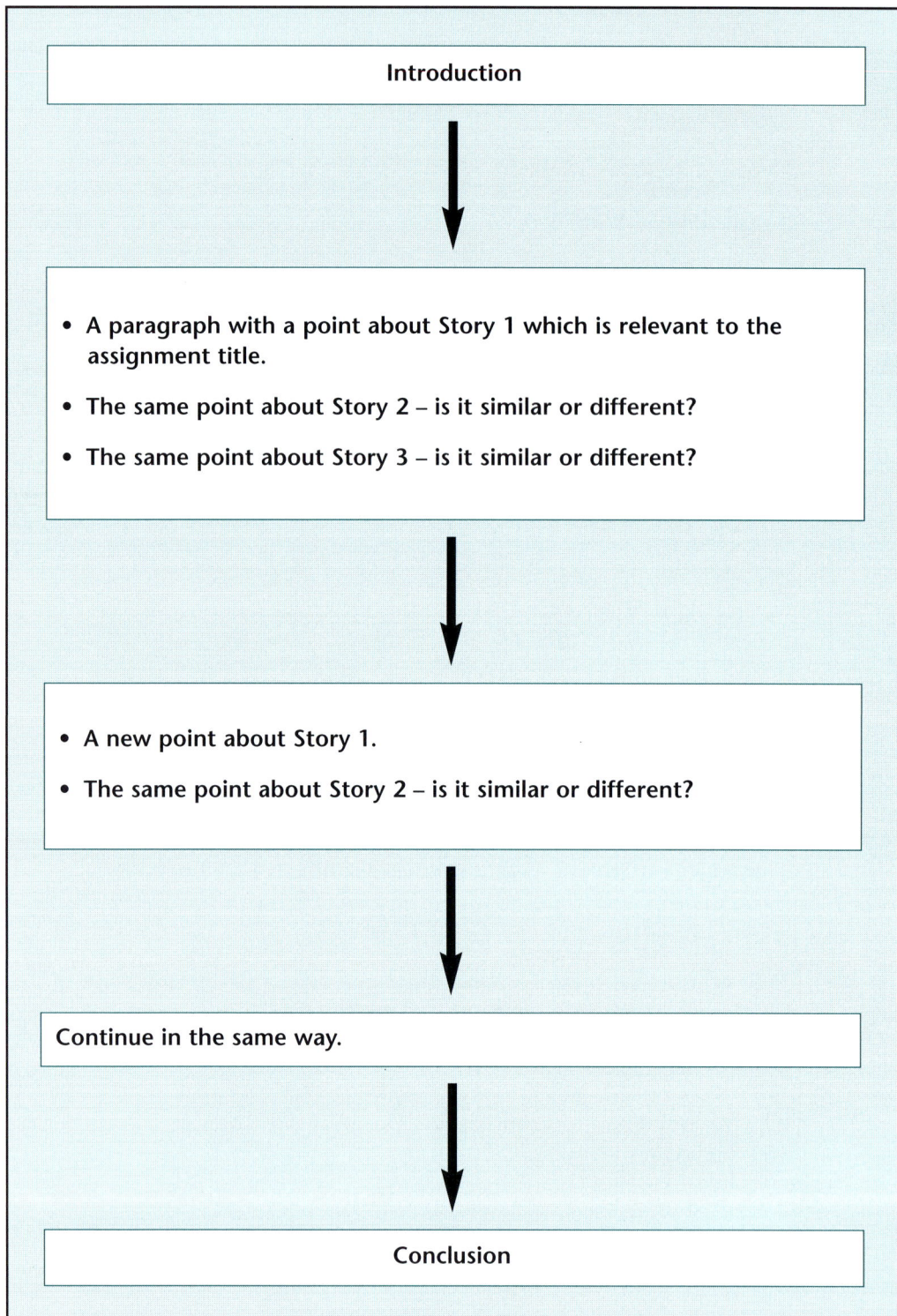

**Introduction**

- A paragraph with a point about Story 1 which is relevant to the assignment title.

- The same point about Story 2 – is it similar or different?

- The same point about Story 3 – is it similar or different?

- A new point about Story 1.

- The same point about Story 2 – is it similar or different?

Continue in the same way.

**Conclusion**

# Planning a comparative essay

When you are writing a comparative essay, it is extremely important to plan. If you just start writing it will be very difficult to keep all the stories in your head, jump between them to make comparisons and make sure you are answering the question fully! See pages 113 and 114 for some help. Here are some planning methods for comparative essays.

## Planning in columns

A simple chart can help you to keep track of similarities and differences. Head each column with the story title. Down the left-hand side put points that would be relevant to the title of your assignment (use the bullet points in the question to help you). As you fill in the chart you will start to notice similarities and differences between the stories. An example has been started for you below on the relationship between Holmes and Watson.

| Relationship between Holmes and Watson | 'A Scandal in Bohemia' | 'Silver Blaze' | 'The Red-Headed League' |
|---|---|---|---|
| Watson as a character | H tells the King: 'You may say before this gentleman anything which you may say to me.' | | H: 'You share my love of all that is bizarre'. |
| Watson as narrator | | | H to W: 'to chronicle, and, if you will excuse my saying so, ... to embellish ... my adventures'. |
| Watson as a plot device | Builds up importance of Irene Adler. | | |
| The way dialogue is used | | | |
| Other points | | | |

## Planning using a Venn diagram

Another way to keep track of similarities and differences is to use a Venn diagram like the one below. In the circle for each story put the elements for that story – in the overlapping sections write the elements that two or more stories have in common. Again, an example has been started for you on whether Holmes is too perfect.

**Is Holmes too perfect?**

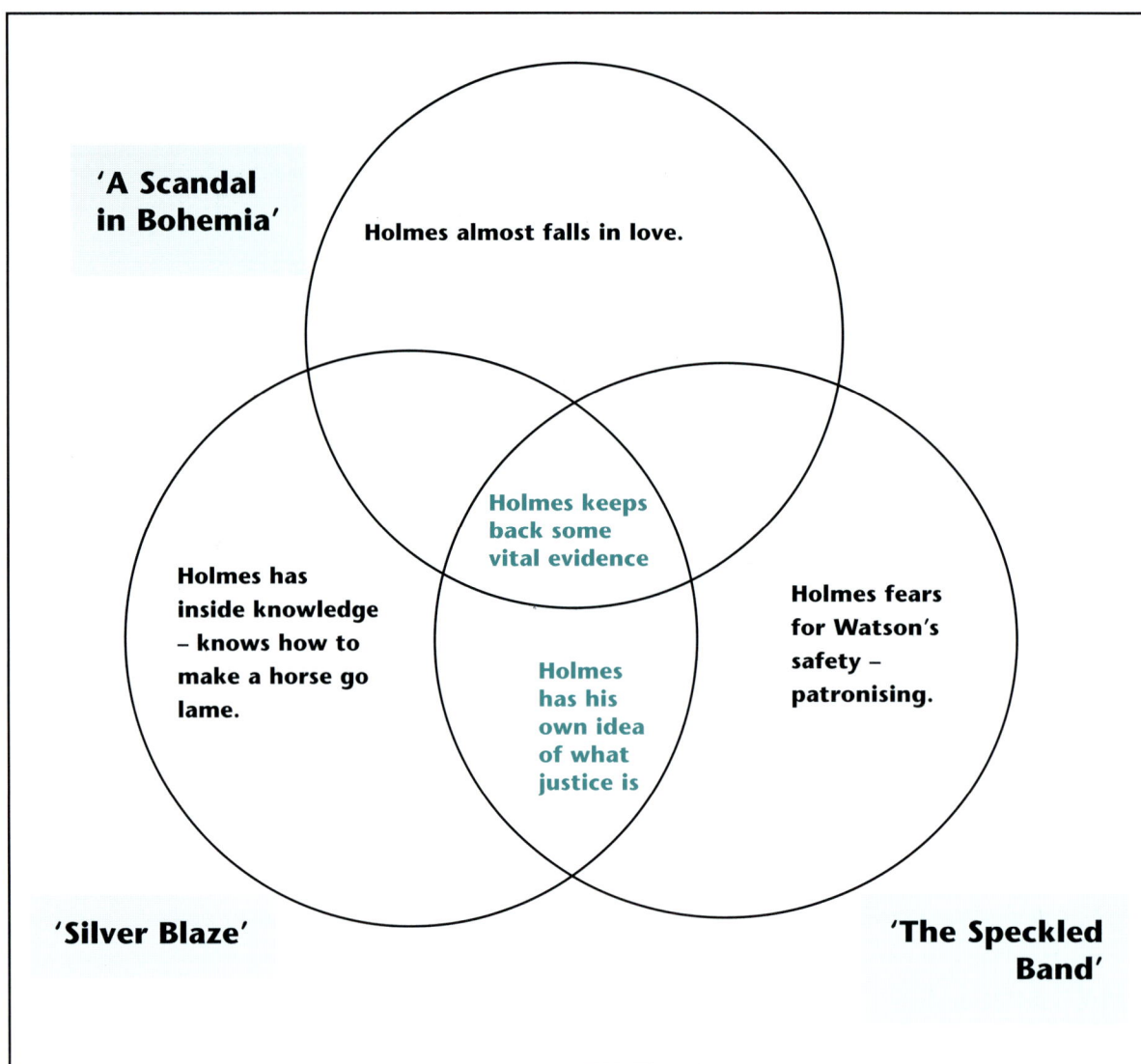

**'A Scandal in Bohemia'**

Holmes almost falls in love.

Holmes keeps back some vital evidence

Holmes has inside knowledge – knows how to make a horse go lame.

Holmes has his own idea of what justice is

Holmes fears for Watson's safety – patronising.

**'Silver Blaze'**

**'The Speckled Band'**

# Drafting and re-drafting

## Linking ideas in your writing

Here are some words and phrases you will find useful for linking ideas in your writing. When you are re-drafting you could use some of these words to make stronger links between points and to 'signpost' your argument more clearly.

---

**Considering possibilities:**

It could be argued that …

Another possibility is …

Another interpretation of … is …

It might be the case that …

One way of looking at this is …

Some people might think …

One way in which …

---

**Discussing similarities and differences:**

However …

Nevertheless …

Alternatively …

On the other hand …

Whereas …

Equally …

Also …

---

# Re-drafting an essay

**Here are some of the changes you could make to improve your essay when you re-draft it. Even when you are mainly being marked for reading, the way you express yourself affects how well you manage to communicate your ideas to your reader.**

## Revise at text level

- Reading your essay aloud can help you to think about the way you have phrased things and to check everything makes sense.

- Make changes to ideas or content, for example, have you covered all aspects of the question? Have you shown a clear overview of all the stories as well as an ability to look in detail at small sections or quotations?

- Make cuts if you find you are repeating yourself, making an irrelevant point, or rambling.

- Change the order of your ideas, for example, to make better links between points when discussing similarities, or a greater contrast between points when discussing differences.

- Make better links between paragraphs. Remember to use link words and phrases (see page 117).

- Make sure you have a good balance of points and quotations – don't overuse quotations. Remember you can use short quotes and you can refer to the text in your own words.

- Try to have an interesting opening, for example, start with a quotation, a question or an interesting idea rather than 'In this essay I am going to …'

- Try to have an interesting conclusion – this is the last thing the reader will read so it will make an impression. When you write your conclusion imagine you have been asked to answer the title in a paragraph. You can include your personal response. You could finish with an interesting thought or a quotation.

## Edit at sentence and word level

- Communicate more clearly by making changes to the order of words in a sentence or the organisation of sentences within a paragraph.

- Think about how you have used quotations – are they always introduced with 'for example …' or have you found other ways to introduce them and sometimes included the quote as part of your sentence?

## Proof read

- Check spelling: read though, underlining any you are unsure about then look up these words. If you often miss basic spellings, try reading backwards so that you don't skip over words.

- Check punctuation. If you find this difficult, try reading aloud or reading with the voice in your head and listening for the pauses.

- Check capital letters.

 

# Prose study assignments

Here are some suggestions for coursework assignments based on the work you have been doing on Sherlock Holmes. Each assignment is followed by page references to direct you to relevant activities.

The chart on page 110 looks at some of the criteria from the GCSE specifications and relates them to the work you have done on Sherlock Holmes. You may find it helpful to look at the chart and think about which questions are relevant to your assignment. If you have a photocopy of the chart you could highlight the relevant questions. If you are hoping for a B grade or above, you should try to answer the extension questions.

## Assignment titles

**1**

**'Holmes is made possible by Watson.' Discuss how far you agree with this statement. You should comment on:**

- the character and personality of Watson and his relationship with Holmes
- Watson as a plot device and as narrator of the stories
- the way Conan Doyle uses the dialogue between Holmes and Watson, including the writer's use of language
- your personal response.

You should also comment on how the stories are affected by the time and place in which they were written, but your comments should be part of your discussion of other things rather than a separate section.

**Most relevant activities:** The role of Watson (pages 62-3); Different ways of looking at Watson (page 63); Different representations of Watson (page 86); The relationship between Holmes and Watson (page 95-6).

**2**

**What is the main pleasure for the reader in reading a Sherlock Holmes story? You should comment on:**

- the reasons people might enjoy crime fiction
- the way the stories are structured
- the characters and settings
- the writer's use of language
- your personal response.

You should also comment on how the stories are affected by the time and place in which they were written, but your comments should be part of your discussion of other things rather than a separate section.

**Most relevant activities:** Conan Doyle's style – description (pages 28-9); The structure of a crime story (page 44); The role of Watson (pages 62-63); Humour in 'The Red-Headed League' (page 64); How does Conan Doyle build up tension and create atmosphere? (page 64); Your personal response – tracing tension in the story (page 79); One of the best Holmes stories? (page 82); Character (pages 83-87); Structure (pages 88-92); Style (pages 95-97); Crime fiction (pages 100-101).

**3**    **'Holmes is too perfect to be realistic so I can't relate to him at all.' Discuss how far you agree with this statement. You should comment on:**

- the character and personality of Holmes and his relationship with Watson
- the way Conan Doyle uses the dialogue between Holmes and Watson, including the writer's use of language
- the effect of having Watson narrate the story (for example the way he keeps back some information)
- Holmes's 'failure' in 'A Scandal in Bohemia'
- your personal response.

You should also comment on how the stories are affected by the time and place in which they were written, but your comments should be part of your discussion of other things rather than a separate section.

**Most relevant activities:** Why does Holmes fail? (pages 45-48); Different ways of looking at Watson (page 63); Holmes's sense of justice (page 81); Character (pages 83-88); How does he do it? (pages 90-92); Point of view (page 93).

**4**    **How successful is Conan Doyle in writing detective fiction that appeals to a modern reader? You should comment on:**

- the reasons people might enjoy crime fiction
- the way the stories are structured
- the characters and settings
- the writer's use of language
- your personal response.

You should also comment on how the stories are affected by the time and place in which they were written, part of your discussion of other things rather than a separate section.

**Most relevant activities:** Conan Doyle's style – description (pages 28-9); The structure of a crime story (page 44); The role of Watson (pages 62-63); Humour in 'The Red-Headed League' (page 64); How does Conan Doyle build up tension and create atmosphere? (page 64); Your personal response – tracing tension in the story (page 79); One of the best Holmes stories? (page 82); Character (pages 83-87); Structure (pages 88-92); Style (pages 95-97); Crime fiction (pages 100-101).

**5**    **How does Conan Doyle create suspense and tension in the Sherlock Holmes stories? You should comment on:**

- how the writer creates atmosphere
- the effect of having the stories narrated by Watson
- the way the stories are structured, including the openings of the stories
- the way clues are revealed.

You should also comment on how the stories are affected by the time and place in which they were written, part of your discussion of other things rather than a separate section.

**Most relevant activities:** The opening of 'Silver Blaze' (page 14); The opening of the story (pages 30-31); The opening of 'The Red-Headed League' (page 50); Your personal response – tracing tension in the story (page 79); How does he do it? (page 90-92); Point of view (page 93).

# Oral assignments

Many specifications offer the option of completing one of your reading/literature assignments as an oral rather than a written piece of coursework. If your teacher decides that you can be assessed in this way you could do one of the following assignments.

**1**

## Jigsaw discussion

In this assignment you will work in a small group to prepare for a discussion. This group is called your 'expert group' and you will prepare together one of the stories you have read. You will then join a new 'discussion group' made up of two or three other people who have prepared different stories. Each of you will give a brief presentation about the story you researched and then you will have a discussion about all the stories you have studied.

When you have a discussion in class, often you do not have much time to prepare, and part of the purpose of the discussion is to work out what you think. However, this discussion is slightly different. In this discussion you need to demonstrate how much you know about Sherlock Holmes and, as well as expressing your opinion, you must refer closely to the stories to support what you say. You will need to spend time researching and preparing. The focus for your discussion is:

**What is the main pleasure for the reader in reading a Sherlock Holmes story? You should comment on:**

- the reasons people might enjoy crime fiction
- the way the stories are structured
- the characters and settings
- the writer's use of language
- your personal response
- you should also comment on how the stories are affected by the time and place in which they were written, but your comments should be part of your discussion of other things rather than a separate section.

**Most relevant activities:** Conan Doyle's style – description (pages 28-9); The structure of a crime story (page 44); The role of Watson (pages 62-63); Humour in 'The Red-Headed League' (page 64); How does Conan Doyle build up tension and create atmosphere? (page 64); Your personal response – tracing tension in the story (page 79); One of the best Holmes stories? (page 82); Character (pages 83-87); Structure (pages 88-92); Style (pages 95-97); Crime fiction (pages 100-101).

---

### Jigsaw Stage 1 – Preparation in Expert Groups of 3

Working in your 'expert' group with two others, you should prepare to answer the question 'What is the main pleasure for the reader in reading a Sherlock Holmes story?' for the story you have been asked to focus on. You could use the questions on the chart on page 110 to help you. In your preparation you should find examples and quotations from the story to support your points. When you have researched together, each person should work alone to produce a short presentation on the story (your presentation should take between one and three minutes).

---

> **Jigsaw Stage 2 – Discussion in New Groups of 3**
>
> Move into your new 'discussion' group with people who have studied different stories.
> Your teacher should appoint a chairperson from a different group. This person does
> not join in the discussion and is not being assessed: their job is to make sure everyone
> gets a chance to speak and to keep the discussion going, by asking questions if
> necessary. Each person should give their presentation. You should then move on to the
> discussion – it will help if one of you asks a question to get things started. If the
> discussion seems to be running out of steam, ask another question (you could use the
> questions from the chart on page 110). Your teacher will tell you when s/he thinks
> they have enough information to grade you and s/he may also ask some questions if
> they think that important points have been missed, or if you are not supporting your
> views with evidence.

## 2 A presentation

**Another way to be assessed orally is to use one of the questions for written
assignments, but to present your ideas as a speech rather than as an essay. Your
presentation could be to the whole class, to a small group, or to your teacher.**

## 3 An interview

**A third way to be assessed orally is to use one of the questions for written
assignments but to prepare for a one-to-one discussion with your teacher who will
then assess you.**

# Original writing assignments

As a result of reading the Sherlock Holmes stories you could write a piece of original writing coursework. If you want to, this could be writing your own detective story. However, you could just use some of the techniques you have learned to do a more focused piece. The following activities can be done separately or you can put the ideas together to write your own detective story.

## Titles

**Usually you would give your story a title after you have written it, or perhaps after you have planned it. However, you could use one of Conan Doyle's titles listed below as a way to get you started.**

A Case of Identity
The Adventure of the Engineer's Thumb
The Second Stain
The Five Orange Pips
The Man with the Twisted Lip
A Study in Scarlet
The Adventure of the Copper Beeches
The Empty House
The Adventure of the Cardboard Box

**You could even write a parody (a humorous imitation) or a typical Holmes story, using Conan Doyle's style and the characters of Watson and Holmes.**

## Creating a character

**Look back at the work you did on the characteristics of a private detective and the advice from Greg Fallis on page 84.**

**Make notes on a detective character of your own who has all or some of these features. You will need to decide:**

- Is your detective male or female?
- How old is your detective?
- What do they look like?
- How do they speak?
- Do they have a sidekick, like Watson?

### Taking it further ...
- What is their favourite piece of music?
- What is their earliest memory?
- What would you find in their pocket or bag?
- What is their greatest fear?
- Who is their closest friend?

**Character assignment – Write the opening of a detective story**

- The detective is relaxing at home alone or with their sidekick. What can you show about this character from the place in which they live?
- He/she looks out of the window and observes someone on the street – what can they tell about the person? Remember Holmes's observation techniques (pages 90-91).
- This person rings the doorbell; it is a new client with a problem.
- The detective interviews the client, finding out as much about the case as they can. Make sure that the client tells their story in an interesting way.
- The detective decides whether or not to take the case. The client leaves. If the detective has a sidekick, s/he should discuss the case with them. Remember how to show character through dialogue – who will ask more questions, and so on (pages 95-96)?

## Creating a setting

Make a map of a location as you did in 'Silver Blaze' (pages 14-15). It should either be a place you know well of somewhere you can easily imagine. On your map, plan what will happen, when and where.

## Taking it further ...

Remind yourself of some of the descriptive techniques you can use to create settings and build up atmosphere (pages 28-29).

**Setting assignment – Describe your detective at the scene of a crime**

Use as many descriptive techniques as you can.

Make sure that you create atmosphere – don't just describe lots of blood and gore.

Have your detective discover some mysterious clues as s/he searches the scene in great detail.

## Putting it all together – Structuring your story

If you would now like to write your own detective story you will need to plan it carefully and think about the structure: remember that at its simplest a detective story can be looked at as shown on page 125.

Coursework – Original writing

**Order**

↓

**Disruption of the order caused by the crime**

↓

**The investigation**

↓

**Order restored**

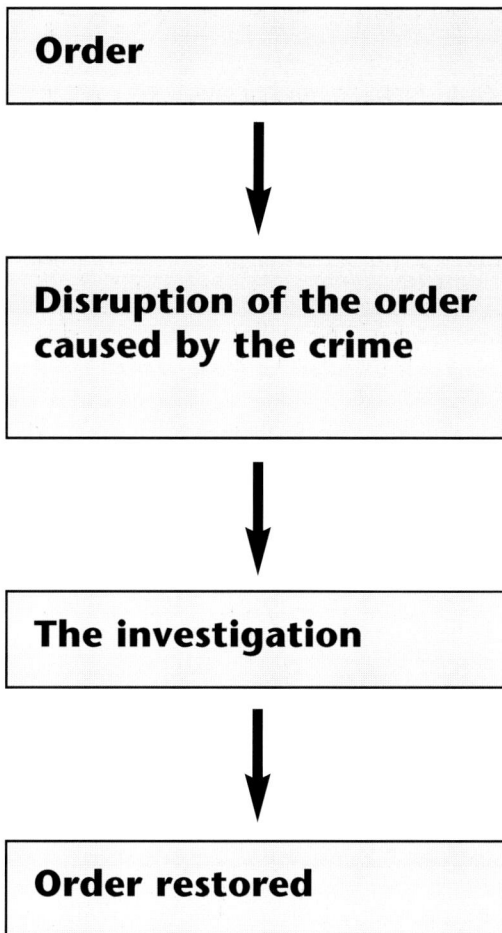

Plan the basic outline of your story using this structure.

Remind yourself of the ingredients Doyle uses (page 89). Which of these could you adapt to use in your story?

## Taking it further ...

Remember how Doyle plans the mystery: think about the key idea, the crime, who commits it, and why. Then consider what clues will give them away and allow the detective to solve the case. Finally, think about how to hide the clues: lay a false trail so that there seems to be another obvious suspect; which elements of the clues could you keep back?

© English & Media Centre, 2004     Studying Sherlock Holmes     **125**

# Further reading

Here are just a few suggestions of crime fiction titles you might enjoy. There is a huge variety within the genre, so if you don't like the first one you try, keep looking! For a much larger list, with book reviews, go to www.crimetime.co.uk/bookreviews.

---

**Linda Barnes**

The Carlotta Carlyle mysteries. Carlotta is a 'gutsy six-foot, red-haired taxi driving private investigator' (for example *Cold Case*).

---

**Laurence Block**

The Matt Scudder series is dark and grim (for example *A Stab in the Dark*). The Bernie Rhodenbarr series is light and comic (for example *The Burglar in the Library*).

---

**Sir Arthur Conan Doyle**      **The Adventures of Sherlock Holmes**

---

**Agatha Christie**

Wrote crime novels from the 1920s, right up to the 1970s. Known for her clue puzzle style novels, featuring Miss Marple or Hercule Poirot, many of which have been made into films or used for television series (for example *The Mysterious Affair at Styles*).

---

**Raymond Chandler**

Wrote in America in the 1930s, 40s and 50s. One of the originators of the 'hard-boiled' genre, which usually features sarcastic, tough detectives and city locations (for example *Farewell, My Lovely*).

---

**Michael Connolly**

Best known for the Harry Bosch series. In the hard-boiled style (for example *Dark Echo*).

---

**Martina Cole**

Featuring feisty DI Kate Burrows (for example *Broken*).

---

**Sara Paretsky**

VI Washawski is Paretsky's feisty female private investigator. Set in Chicago (for example *Ghost Country*).

## Jeffery Deaver

Deaver's gruesome novels feature quadriplegic criminalist Lincoln Rhyme (for example *The Coffin Dancer*).

## Janet Evanovitch

The novels are lively and funny and feature Stephanie Plum, a bail-bondswoman (for example *One for the Money*).

## Sue Grafton

Her popular female private investigator works her way through the alphabet -– the first book in the series was *A is for Alibi* and the most recent is *Q is for Quarry*.

## William Gibson

Best known as a science fiction writer, some of his books are also crime fiction (for example *Idoru* and its sequel *All Tomorrow's Parties*). Set in the near future in a high-tech world.

## Carl Hiassen

Very funny, in a rather dark way (for example *Native Tongue*).

## Reginald Hill

The Dalziel and Pascoe series were made into a television series. Set in Yorkshire (for example *On Beulah Height*).

## Patricia Highsmith

The Ripley series are written from the point of view of the criminal. Two of these novels have recently been made into films (for example *The Talented Mr Ripley*).

## Chester Himes

Himes wrote his first book featuring African American detectives Coffin Ed Johnson and Grave Digger Jones in 1945 while he was in prison for armed robbery (for example *Rage in Harlem*).

## Peter May

May's detective is Chinese and the books are set in Beijing (for example *The Runner*).

## Walter Mosely

Mosely's first novel, *Devil in a Blue Dress*, was made into a film starring Denzel Washington as reluctant private investigator Easy Rawlins.

# Answers

## Holmes's deductions from the clues on page 10

Holmes deduces…

From clue 1. …that the footprints were made by a tall man who limps with the right leg. He also deduces that the murderer was left-handed and that the stone was probably the murder weapon as it obviously hadn't been there long.

From clue 2. … that the woman is coming to see him about a problem in a relationship – her hesitation shows that she wants advice but is not sure whether the problem is too private to discuss with a stranger. He says that the woman is not so much angry with the man involved as puzzled or upset – if she were angry she would not have hesitated.

From clue 3. … that the woman left home in a great hurry.

## Solution to the locked room mystery on page 66

Answer: the woman stood on a block of ice from the freezer to reach the noose. The ice began to melt and then finally collapsed, leaving her hanging from the rope.